# In Search of Our
# ANCESTORS

## 101 Inspiring Stories of
## Serendipity and Connection
## in Rediscovering Our
## Family History

Megan Smolenyak

△

Adams Media Corporation
Holbrook, Massachusetts

*To Stacy Smolenyak Shields Neuberger—*
*I'm so grateful our ancestors conspired to make you my sister!*

∾

Copyright ©2000, Megan Smolenyak. All rights reserved.
This book, or parts thereof, may not be reproduced in any
form without permission from the publisher; exceptions are made for
brief excerpts used in published reviews.

Published by
Adams Media Corporation
260 Center Street, Holbrook, MA 02343. U.S.A.

ISBN: 1-58062-317-4
Printed in Canada.

J I H G F E D C B A

**Library of Congress Cataloging-in-Publication Data**
In search of our ancestors : 101 inspiring stories of serendipity and
connection in rediscovering our family history / [compiled] by Megan Smolenyak.
p.      cm.
A companion book to the PBS television series Ancestors.
ISBN 1-58062-317-4
1. United States—Genealogy—Anecdotes. 2. Genealogy—Anecdotes.
I. Smolenyak, Megan.
CS16I4                    2000
929'.1'072073--dc21        99-087248
                           CIP

This publication is designed to provide accurate and authoritative information with regard to the subject matter covered. It is sold with the understanding that the publisher is not engaged in rendering legal, accounting, or other professional advice. If legal advice or other expert assistance is required, the services of a competent professional person should be sought.
— From a *Declaration of Principles* jointly adopted by a Committee of the American Bar Association and a Committee of Publishers and Associations

The "See It On PBS" logo is a trademark of
the Public Broadcasting Service and is used with permission.

Photo on page 13 (also appearing on front cover), courtesy of Eva Butler.
Photo on page 82 (also appearing on rear cover), courtesy of Lynne K. Ranieri.
Photos on page 176 (also appearing on front cover), 178 and 179, ©2000, Bobbye Dones.
Photo on page 187 (also appearing on front cover), courtesy of Carin Van Vooren.
Photo of great-grandmother and babies appearing front cover, courtesy of Beth Uyehara.
Photo of class play appearing rear cover, courtesy of Megan Smolenyak.

All other photos appearing on front cover and spine ©Index Stock Imagery.

*This book is available at quantity discounts for bulk purchases.*
*For information, call 1-800-872-5627.*

**Visit our exciting Web site: www.adamsmedia.com**

# Contents

Introduction . . . . . . . . . . . . . . . . . . . . . . . . . . . . . . . . . . .vii

Part One: Providence in Action . . . . . . . . . . . . . . . . .1
   Grave Matters. . . . . . . . . . . . . . . . . . . . . . . . . . . . . . . 3
   Wrong Number. . . . . . . . . . . . . . . . . . . . . . . . . . . . . 6
   She Wanted Herself Known . . . . . . . . . . . . . . . . . . 7
   A Little Prayer Goes a Long Way . . . . . . . . . . . . . . 10
   Market Instincts . . . . . . . . . . . . . . . . . . . . . . . . . . . 12
   An Unbreakable Bond. . . . . . . . . . . . . . . . . . . . . . . 14
   In Her Footsteps. . . . . . . . . . . . . . . . . . . . . . . . . . . 16
   The Benefits of Lost Luggage . . . . . . . . . . . . . . . . . 18
   Mother's Last Gift . . . . . . . . . . . . . . . . . . . . . . . . . 20
   Dancing Ghosts . . . . . . . . . . . . . . . . . . . . . . . . . . . 22
   Always Listen to Your Mother! . . . . . . . . . . . . . . . 24
   I Just Had to Go to Germany . . . . . . . . . . . . . . . . . 26
   What Made Me Say That? . . . . . . . . . . . . . . . . . . . 28
   I Will Always Love You. . . . . . . . . . . . . . . . . . . . . . 29
   A Prophetic Doodle . . . . . . . . . . . . . . . . . . . . . . . . 31
   Meeting over Coffee. . . . . . . . . . . . . . . . . . . . . . . . 32

Part Two: Connecting with Kin . . . . . . . . . . . . . . . .35
   Ever Changing . . . . . . . . . . . . . . . . . . . . . . . . . . . . 37
   A Class-ic Connection . . . . . . . . . . . . . . . . . . . . . . 39
   Looking for Margaret . . . . . . . . . . . . . . . . . . . . . . . 41
   More than Names on a Chart . . . . . . . . . . . . . . . . . 43
   A Fresh Branch. . . . . . . . . . . . . . . . . . . . . . . . . . . . 45
   Lost Americans. . . . . . . . . . . . . . . . . . . . . . . . . . . . 46
   Cherished . . . . . . . . . . . . . . . . . . . . . . . . . . . . . . . . 48
   Miss Universe . . . . . . . . . . . . . . . . . . . . . . . . . . . . . 51
   The French Connection . . . . . . . . . . . . . . . . . . . . . 53
   She Deserves to Know . . . . . . . . . . . . . . . . . . . . . . 56

Honeymoon Surprise . . . . . . . . . . . . . . . . . . . . . . . . . . . .58
It Pays to Advertise . . . . . . . . . . . . . . . . . . . . . . . . . . . . .61
Probably Your Cousin . . . . . . . . . . . . . . . . . . . . . . . . . . . .62
A Strong Hold . . . . . . . . . . . . . . . . . . . . . . . . . . . . . . . .64
The Perils of Genealogy . . . . . . . . . . . . . . . . . . . . . . . . . .66
The Brother She Never Knew . . . . . . . . . . . . . . . . . . . . . .67
Is That You, Robbie? . . . . . . . . . . . . . . . . . . . . . . . . . . . .69
Revitalizing the Family Tree . . . . . . . . . . . . . . . . . . . . . .71

Part Three: If at First You Don't Succeed . . . . . . . . .75
Genetealogy . . . . . . . . . . . . . . . . . . . . . . . . . . . . . . . . . .77
Ask and You Shall Receive . . . . . . . . . . . . . . . . . . . . . . .79
Righting Old Wrongs . . . . . . . . . . . . . . . . . . . . . . . . . . . .80
Pots and Clans . . . . . . . . . . . . . . . . . . . . . . . . . . . . . . . .82
A 4,000 Year Family Tradition . . . . . . . . . . . . . . . . . . . .85
A Useful Dees-Tour . . . . . . . . . . . . . . . . . . . . . . . . . . . .88
Tombstone Detective . . . . . . . . . . . . . . . . . . . . . . . . . . .90
Where Did All the Flemings Go? . . . . . . . . . . . . . . . . . .94
Serendipity and Persistence . . . . . . . . . . . . . . . . . . . . . .96
Digging for Roots . . . . . . . . . . . . . . . . . . . . . . . . . . . . . .98
Dusty Memories . . . . . . . . . . . . . . . . . . . . . . . . . . . . . .102
Diary of a Diary Quest . . . . . . . . . . . . . . . . . . . . . . . . .105
As Clear as Mud . . . . . . . . . . . . . . . . . . . . . . . . . . . . . .109
The Traveling Bible . . . . . . . . . . . . . . . . . . . . . . . . . . . .112
Looking for Love . . . . . . . . . . . . . . . . . . . . . . . . . . . . . .115
Little White Lies . . . . . . . . . . . . . . . . . . . . . . . . . . . . . .117
Children of Manchester . . . . . . . . . . . . . . . . . . . . . . . . .119

Part Four: The Kindness of Strangers . . . . . . . . . .131
Memorial Day Is Every Day . . . . . . . . . . . . . . . . . . . . .133
Reclaimed Freight . . . . . . . . . . . . . . . . . . . . . . . . . . . . .136
What's in a Name? . . . . . . . . . . . . . . . . . . . . . . . . . . . . .138
An Honest Broker . . . . . . . . . . . . . . . . . . . . . . . . . . . . .140
Let Me Explain . . . . . . . . . . . . . . . . . . . . . . . . . . . . . . .142
Cellar Treasure . . . . . . . . . . . . . . . . . . . . . . . . . . . . . . .144

Recaptured History ...........................147
Perfect Timing ..............................150
Newsworthy ................................152
Pass It On .................................153
Worth the Wait .............................154
A Restorative Hobby .........................156
Crossing State Lines .........................159
Bi-Coastal Bible ............................160
Making a Present of the Past ..................163
Rummaging for Relatives .....................165
Gone but Not Forgotten ......................167

**Part Five: Breaking the Time Barrier ...........169**
Sunbonnet Sue...............................171
Boom-Boom Ugarrio ........................174
Standing Tall ...............................176
Dated Discovery.............................180
A Dash of Larceny ..........................181
Island of Tears .............................184
Apron Strings...............................187
Surveying across the Centuries..................190
The Picture on the Wall ......................191
Robert's Legacy .............................193
Finding My Father ...........................195
Just What I Wanted ..........................198
Mistaken Identity ...........................200
Pass to Freedom.............................202
Sacred Memories............................204
A Forgotten Treasure ........................205

**Part Six: What Were the Odds? ................207**
A Really Good Friday .........................209
Split-Second Timing .........................210
Home Again ...............................212
Small World ...............................214

Blind Luck Can Lead You Home .................. 216
It Just Showed Up ............................ 218
Postcard Guard............................... 220
Welcome Interruption.......................... 222
Signs of Illness .............................. 223
Christmas Present............................. 224
Serendipity Delayed .......................... 226
Careful Where You Look!....................... 228
A Different Kind of Valentine's Day .............. 229
Restoring a Sampler Restored My Family........... 231
Timing Is Everything ......................... 233
Copier Cousins............................... 235
Blooming Ink ................................ 236

Permissions ................................. 239
Acknowledgments ............................ 241

# Introduction

*To trace lineage, to love and record the names and actions of those without whom we never could have been, who moulded and made us what we are, and whom the very greatest of all must know to have propagated influences into his being which must subtly but certainly act upon his whole conduct in this world, all this is implied in ancestry and the love of it, and it is natural and good.*

—WESTMINISTER REVIEW, JULY 1823

I couldn't agree more with the person who wrote these words. From my three decades as a genealogist, I too have come away with the belief that no matter how much we might try to ignore or even deny our roots, they claim us in ways we don't even know. When we search for our ancestors, we honor them through our efforts, but doing so is as much for our own benefit as for theirs.

For instance, when I was younger, I fancied that I was the first world traveler in my family; that is, until I came across a photo of my grandmother, mother, and me at Versailles in France when I was all of three weeks old. Hmmm . . . maybe I wasn't the first after all.

I delved back into my genealogy looking for evidence concerning this particular aspect of "my" personality. What I learned is that I am, at a minimum, a sixth-generation vagabond. Not only was I not the first; it was virtually inevitable. By exploring my family's past, I had learned more about myself.

All of us have these invisible imprints inherited from previous generations, and more and more of us are making the attempt to learn about them. Our motivations may vary, but it is clear that genealogy is enjoying explosive growth for a combination of reasons that suggest we "ain't seen nothing yet."

Some seek self-knowledge. Others dabble innocently and get pulled in the same way one gets sucked into a good mystery novel, for genealogy is essentially a detective game with its clues scattered around the globe. The Internet makes it possible for many novices to quickly stumble onto information about their families, and a taste of instant gratification almost always produces another addict.

Those whose Southern and Eastern European grandparents and great-grandparents were part of the massive immigration wave into the Americas and Australia around the last turn of the century are now far enough removed from the old country to become curious about their roots. This timing is rather convenient as many of the relevant records for these ethnic groups just became accessible in the 1990s.

Still others have religious motivations, and of course, there's the aging of the baby boom generation. It's true that genealogy can provide a tiny piece of immortality, and that this might offer a partial explanation for its popularity with "older" people. But there's also the more practical explanation that retired folks have the time it takes to actively pursue genealogy.

Add to all this the fact that changing millennia seems to have put many of us into reflective and nostalgic moods, and you have a recipe for roots mania.

So is all this genealogical enthusiasm truly "natural and good," as the anonymous writer quoted earlier asserts? Just try convincing millions of genealogists otherwise!

We do indeed honor our ancestors when we search for them, and it seems, they return the favor! As virtually any longtime genealogist will tell you, when one makes the effort to learn about the lives of ancestors, they will often meet you halfway.

What does this mean? Simply that there is far too much coincidence in genealogy to be explained away as such. In fact, the word *coincidence* is dangerously close to losing its meaning. As with the seriously overworked *awesome*, sheer repetition has stripped the word of its original intent.

I was fortunate enough to be part of the team that produced the PBS series *Ancestors*. When we embarked on research for the show, all of us were struck by a common theme that threaded its way through the majority of the stories we considered. People have different names for it—luck, serendipity, Spirit, synchronicity, God, intuition—but whatever you call it, *it* exists. There's clearly something larger than mere coincidence at work and genealogists experience it every day.

How else can you explain the following:

~ All the distant cousins, now living thousands of miles apart, who have met when "coincidentally" visiting the cemetery of their ancestors on the same day

~ All the seemingly off-topic books that call to researchers who finally find that missing clue within their pages

~ All the family treasures—photos, papers, and Bibles—that are reunited with their original families under circumstances that boggle the mind

~ All the rolls of microfilm that magically scroll to exactly the right page with the long-sought information

~ All the genealogists who literally trip over their ancestors' graves when confronted with a massive cemetery overflowing with tombstones

In fact, so immersed did we become in this sea of serendipity that it began to happen to us as we worked on the series. Imagine the surprise of Utah-based producer Craig Steiner when an apartment in New York City—now how many of them can there be?—selected by a locations firm for the taping of one segment turned out to belong to his second cousin Lorinda. It seemed only appropriate.

Several other themes emerged during the course of our research. We found ourselves engulfed in tales of generosity, connection, and creativity, even though this is not what we had originally set out to find.

It would almost seem that the phenomenon of random acts of kindness began with genealogy. The genealogical community is a refreshingly generous one, and we found story after story of complete strangers helping each other. Many involve Internet acquaintances who assist each other simply because they can. Others have restored cemeteries, painstakingly transcribed old records, or created free on-line databases of hard-to-access information—all without any expectation of compensation or reward.

We marveled at how genealogy brings people together. Adoptees use genealogical techniques to find their birth families, even if scattered to other continents. Second, third, fourth, even tenth cousins find each other and feel an instant kinship, even though their blood connection may have been three centuries ago. Researchers reconstruct the lives of special ancestors who somehow call to them a little more loudly than the others and develop a bond as strong as if the person were alive today.

We were also dazzled by the creativity and persistence of genealogists. All researchers encounter brick walls, but who knew there were so many ways to get over them? A tombstone was stolen twenty years ago? No problem. A genealogist is on the case and will rescue the errant stone. The records don't go back far enough? Not an obstacle. A genealogist will talk scientists into conducting a DNA experiment to make the connections that the documents can't.

So here was our dilemma: We were swimming in wonderful genealogical tales, but could only squeeze so many into the series. It pained us that so many worthy stories were going untold. Our solution was to share as many as we could in this, the companion book to the series.

In these pages, you'll find the stories featured in *Ancestors*, as well as a number of others that captured our imaginations. You'll find a surprising variety of stories of serendipity and connection that occurred when people sought to learn more about their family history.

We hope these tales will capture your imagination, and better yet, that *you* will experience serendipity and find connections in your own search for your ancestors.

# PART ONE

# Providence in Action

$\mathcal{I}$f you were to gather fifty genealogists in a room, chances are that forty-five of them would readily admit to having experienced a few unexplainable incidents in their search for roots. With a little time and reflection, the other five would probably 'fess up as well. Most often, this takes the form of intuition or "that little voice that just told me to _____." Fill in the blank however you'd like: look at that book, talk to that woman, get off at that exit, open that drawer.

Genealogists are great detectives and learn to trust their hunches even when there is no logical reason to do so. Time and time again, they are rewarded for listening to this inner voice. They find the missing clue, the family Bible, the old homestead, or the long-lost cousin.

This happens so frequently and in such unlikely ways that it seems we must be getting some help. People have different interpretations and a variety of names for it; but for purposes of simplicity, let's just call it "providence."

This providential assistance comes in other forms as well. It could be a chance encounter, a document that survived unharmed in spite of fire or flood, or a long-shot prayer that's answered on the spot. As you read the following tales, see if one or two don't bring to mind an "unexplainable" event that's happened to you or someone you know.

# Grave Matters

*W*hen I began genealogical research, I discovered that it's just as important to be lucky as to be smart. Maybe even more so. I've also heard people say that it pays to be nice to our ancestors as we go along.

Three years ago, after just starting research, I decided I was ready for my first genealogical field trip. I headed to Pennsylvania from my home in California, armed with unbounded ignorance and optimism and what turned out to be a remarkable streak of beginner's luck.

In Schuylkill County, I managed to locate my great-grandfather's grave. In triumph, I headed to town, and staggered back to the cemetery with the largest basket of blooms I could afford.

The next morning at the courthouse, while looking through deed indexes, I accidentally grabbed a book from the wrong shelf, and opened an index from the 1920s—decades after my family had left the area. Before noticing my "mistake," I found two quit-claim deeds signed by all my great-grandfather's descendants and their spouses, showing their relationships and cities of residence. The deeds also revealed the name of a mystery great-great-grand-father. It was a bonanza of information, and remains one of my major finds.

It was nothing but sheer, dumb luck. Or was it the flowers? Hmmm.

From there, I headed west a few hundred miles to research another line. At the Clearfield County Historical Society, I learned where another great-grandfather was likely to be buried. When I found his grave, his old, marble headstone was leaning at a dan-gerous angle, ready to topple. So in addition to buying flowers, I

*The tombstone of Benjamin Ellis as it was found, leaning right and forward.*

called a local monument company and arranged for the stone to be repaired and straightened.

I was positive that Great-Grandpa had not lived long enough after immigrating to apply for citizenship, but on my way out of town, I stopped at the courthouse anyway. I asked the woman at the counter about 1870s naturalization records. She pulled out a little index box, and there was his name. She found his file, and inside were not only his final certificate of citizenship, but also his personal copy of the Declaration of Intention. He must have left it behind at his swearing-in as a citizen. Since he had died just twelve days after becoming a citizen, he had never returned to pick it up—and there it sat for 120 years. "This belonged to him," the clerk said handing it to me. "We have our own copy. Why don't you keep it?"

As we examined the file together, she gave a little gasp. "Good heavens," she said, "that's *my* great-grandfather's signature." Her ancestor had been the character witness for my ancestor when he applied for citizenship, so they had obviously been friends. We stared at each other, then hugged and exchanged family information and names and addresses, promising to write, which we have done.

The genealogical kicker to all this is that the certificate included Great-Grandpa's date of immigration and port of entry, which I had not known before.

When I left the courthouse, I headed thirty miles back to the cemetery, instead of to the turnpike. Feeling slightly foolish, I patted the wobbly old stone and whispered, "Hey, I just met your old pal Richard's great-granddaughter. And I found the Declaration you left behind. I'm going to frame it and pass it along to future generations." And I added as I left, "Thanks!"

As I say, you can't beat dumb luck. As for the flowers, I have a sneaking suspicion that they helped, too!

—*Beth Uyehara, California*

*Benjamin Ellis's grave stone standing*
*tall and erect after repairs.*

# Wrong Number

*M*y dear aunt was trying to help me locate family contacts and "thought this was the right listing" in the phone book. I was not overly surprised, then, when the elderly man who answered informed me I had the wrong number. He wanted to be helpful and called his wife to the phone.

I thought it was pretty pointless, but told her my purpose and began listing family names. "No, no, I don't know any of them," she replied. "Wait, what was that last one? Oh yes, my father used to work for that family. You need to talk to Elsie in Atlantic City. She's one of the daughters."

Could it be that a random stranger might have tripped across my family in the past? I found a listing for Elsie and called her. To my amazement, she was indeed a distant cousin and had collected information tracing that family branch back to the 1600s in Switzerland! Pretty good results for a "wrong" number—or what I prefer to think of providence at work!

—*Carol Glynn, Texas*

# She Wanted
# Herself Known

*O*ne day, when I was in the third grade, we were studying the Bible in school. Sister Whilemenha was sitting at the front of the room, reading us a long list of "begats."

Abraham begat Isaac. Isaac begat Jacob. So-and-so begat so-and-so. After several minutes of this, I raised my hand and asked her why they never begat any girl children in the Bible.

"Oh, they had girl children," Sister said. "They just weren't important enough to write their names down."

Over in the corner, Danny O'Brien snickered. "Girls aren't important," he sneered.

I sat down in my chair with a thud, thinking of all those baby girls, all those mothers, all those grandmothers, not recorded, not remembered, as though they had never existed at all. "Girls aren't important!" Danny taunted, and my face burned.

I thought of Danny one day recently when I was working on my family tree. I knew my ancestors had come from Ireland, but never knew when they came or what part they had come from. When I asked my mother and aunts, they didn't know either, so I visited the archives at Boston City Hall. I thought I'd look for an hour or so to see what I could find.

Pouring over the dusty books in the archives, I found my mother's birth certificate and her parents' marriage certificate. As I traced the faded handwritten names with my finger—James and Catherine Moran—a shiver ran down my spine. Before I knew it, the archives were closing for the day and I had a long list of names to investigate. I was hooked.

I went to the National Archives and the Boston Public Library. I became a detective. Within a few weeks, I had traced part of the family—the Nashes—back to 1863 when they left Tipperary for New York.

When I told the family what I'd found, I discovered there was a vague rumor that my mother's father was adopted. No one really knew for sure; but if the rumor was true, then my family tree was at a dead end unless I could find his birth parents. I was determined to find the truth.

At the library, I poured over the 1880 census records and gasped when I saw the entry for the Morans. The four-year-old James Moran was listed as "Michael James," a nephew. His sister, Mary, was a niece. That meant the old family rumors were true! The children were adopted, but not from strangers. They were a niece and nephew. I should be able to find their parents!

Back at City Hall, I could find no birth certificate for Michael James. I knew my grandfather was born on January 3, 1876, but I didn't know his last name at birth. In 1876, the entries were all handwritten, listed according to family name. "You'll have to go through each entry individually," the woman at the archives said; but it was clear that even she considered this a daunting task. There were nearly eleven thousand babies born in Boston in 1876. The search could take days! I might misread someone's handwriting. I might miss the entry altogether!

I sighed as I opened the dusty book, and flipped through the pages. I looked idly at the names on page 525, then noticed entry number 10,881. "January 3, Michael J.," it said. "Here's a Michael J. born on January 3," I said to the woman.

"Maybe that's the one," she laughed. I laughed too as I read across the page. "Father's name, Michael Naughtin," it said. "Mother's maiden name, Anna Moran." Anna Moran! The name practically leaped off the page. My hands shook as I gripped the book.

By the end of the day, I knew the story. Michael James was born on January 3, 1876, to Anna Moran Naughtin and Michael Naughtin. Anna died of hepatitis in December of that year at the age of twenty-eight. Her children were taken in by her brother, who raised them as his own, naming them James and Mary Moran. I could find no further record of the children's father.

As I left the archives and headed home, I walked slowly. My heart was heavy, as though there had been a recent death in the family. The fact that it happened more than a hundred years ago makes it no less sad to me today.

Anna haunts me. She lived. She bore two children. She died. But if it were not for my digging through the records at City Hall, like so many women before her, we never would have known she existed.

What are the odds that I would open the book to that page and see that record? A thousand to one? A million to one? It was amazing. It was a miracle. "You found that record because Anna wanted herself known," the woman at the archives said. I believe she did.

—*Cathy Corcoran, Massachusetts*

# A Little Prayer
# Goes a Long Way

Several years ago I found an account of a legal matter involving my ancestor, Rufus Walker, in a journal. I traced the source of the item to Blackfoot, Idaho, and wrote to the courthouse there requesting information on the original court records. The officials replied that they knew they had such a record, but it had been misplaced during a recent move to a new building. This was not the news I had hoped to hear, but at least they were kind enough to invite me to come search for it. So that's exactly what I decided to do.

When my husband and I arrived, we were taken to a large basement room with rows and rows of old records. Uh-oh. I knew it would be a search, but I hadn't realized the scope. Not knowing where to begin, we prayed, and started digging through book after book. After some time, we hadn't found any evidence of the court hearing involving Rufus Walker.

Seeking guidance, I bowed my head in prayer once again, and then walked to the most remote row of books. I picked up the last volume on the shelf and read its title: *Records of Marks and Brands*. This didn't look promising, but I opened it anyway. Inside, I discovered that the apparently mislabeled book had been used to record early territorial court hearings. I tried not to get my hopes up too high, but after some frantic page turning, there it was! My ancestor's hearing was the fourth one!

I was thrilled and asked my husband to go upstairs to get a clerk to help us make copies. Now in the basement by myself, I got an overwhelming feeling that I wasn't actually alone. I prayed silently a third time to be led to any additional information about Rufus, and found myself drawn to another row where I plucked out a book at random. Flipping to the index page, I saw the magical listing I was hoping for: "Rufus Walker, page 10."

Turning to that page, I found a record of a later court matter I had no knowledge of. A second unexpected treasure buried in this vast room had all but jumped into my hands! After that experience, I am convinced that we are not alone in the work of searching out our ancestors. It was an incontrovertible sign to me that Rufus truly is interested and cares about the hundreds of hours I have spent reconstructing his lineage.

—*Cheryl Harmon Bean, Idaho*

# Market Instincts

*I*'ve never been a big fan of flea markets. Looking at other people's used stuff is not my idea of a good time. That's why I resisted when I was struck with the notion of going to one close to my home. This feeling badgered me for about a week, but each time, I managed to talk myself out of it. Still the urge persisted.

If only to stop the internal nagging, I finally relented and ventured to the nearby market. Nothing was jumping out at me as I meandered through the buildings, but I found myself lingering at the booths with photographs. Even so, I didn't find any enticing enough to buy.

After a few hours, there was just one booth remaining. I glanced through a pile of old pictures and postcards and turned to go. Several hours in the heat had taken its toll and I was ready to leave, but at the last second, something registered in my brain. I turned back for a second look.

*One of the Cohoctah, Michigan train station photographs found at the flea market.*

*Schuyler Wriggelsworth, second from left in back row,
with his family in 1888.*

On top of the pile next to the one I had already explored was a
picture of a familiar face—my mother-in-law! She had passed
away several years earlier, but there was no mistaking the young
woman staring out from the photo. There she was with her
brothers and parents! I dug deeper and discovered more photos of
her family, her tiny hometown of Cohoctah, the family's house,
and the local train station. My husband's grandfather, with the
impressive name of Schuyler Wriggelsworth, had worked in the
train station, and my mother-in-law often told me of the times
when the children in the family would get out of bed, cross the
road, and sleep in the boxcars to enjoy the evening breeze. Here it
was all brought back to life by this cluster of old photographs that
had somehow found their way to this booth.

Since this episode, I am a flea market convert! Several subsequent finds have convinced me that this "hobby" is not as much
my idea as someone else's who leads me to these scattered clues to
my family's past. It's not the most methodical research technique,
but it sure works for me!

—*Eva Butler, Michigan*

# An Unbreakable Bond

*I*n 1990, I was in a computer store buying some parts when I bumped into somebody. I looked up to say "excuse me" and saw the most intensely beautiful eyes looking right into my soul. Right away, Stephen and I knew we were destined to remain together.

We had so much in common that we hardly noticed that it was a bit of a coincidence that we both had grandmothers who had been avid genealogists and had left us with our respective maternal genealogies back to the 1600s. But this piece of trivia aroused the curiosity of Kate Connolly, a friend of Stephen's and also a keen family historian. She asked to have a look at the genealogies our grandmothers had given to us, and we saw no reason not to indulge her request.

A week before we were to be married in 1993, Kate called and said, "Is Stephen there? Sit down. You gotta hear this. You guys are distant cousins!"

She told us how our grandmothers' papers revealed that our families were friends who had come over from England together on the same ship—the *Zouch Phenix*—to Massachusetts in 1624. Stephen's family name was Balch and mine was Gardner. After the two families arrived in America, Benjamin Balch and Sarah Gardner were married!

Kate sketched a simple chart showing the generations leading down to Stephen and me, making it easy to see that we were tenth cousins once removed. Receiving this news just before our wedding made it even more meaningful to us. Our ancestors had married on the shores of a new world and we were now embarking on a new beginning more than 350 years later, rekindling the bond that had quietly connected our families all these years.

We did not know then how brief our time together was to be. My husband died of cancer at the age of forty-six only three years after our wedding. He was a cinematographer and it was his dream to make an epic tale of the reunion of our families.

It's been over three years since Stephen died, but we're together every day, all day long. Our bond was there before we even knew each other, and it will be there forever.

—*Kim Anderson, Florida*

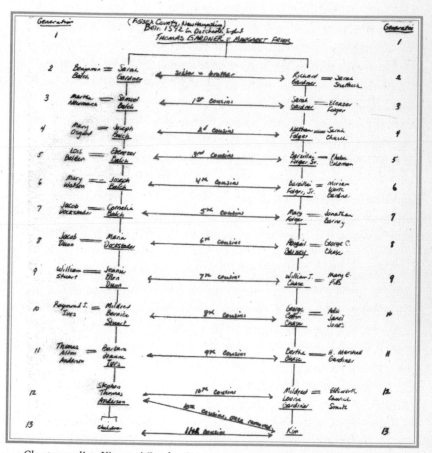

*Chart revealing Kim and Stephen's connection stemming from the marriage of Benjamin Balch and Sarah Gardner (generation 2) in the early 1600s.*

# In Her Footsteps

*M*y great-great-grandmother, Elisabeth Merklin, was ship-wrecked in Key West on her voyage from Germany to New Orleans. According to family tradition, she stayed in Key West and married her rescuer, Peter Thomas Knight, a young mariner from England, in 1849.

On a visit to Key West from my home state of Washington, I went with one of my cousins to see the graves of Elisabeth and Peter Knight. Afterward, we stopped at the cemetery's office to look through the records to see if they held any fresh clues to our family history. While we were there, a couple walked in and asked for assistance. I couldn't help but overhear as the woman told the sexton that they were searching for the graves of Elisabeth Merklin and Peter T. Knight! Of course, I had to interject. Liz, it was revealed, was descended from Elisabeth's third marriage, while I am descended from her first marriage to Peter Knight.

It's peculiar enough that Liz and I should meet in the sexton's office while on the same quest on the same day, but what made this chance meeting even more extraordinary is that Liz was visiting the United States from Germany, where she and her husband were working for the Army. This last fact turned out to be a lucky break for both of us.

As a result of this meeting, I shared the research I had already done with Liz. When she returned to Germany, she used her new knowledge to locate the village in Baden where Elisabeth Merklin was born. A trip to the village happily led to a priest who generously lent Liz the Ortsippenbusch, a book detailing all the births, marriages, and deaths of the parish, giving both of us buckets of new information on our common heritage.

How convenient that my newfound cousin was now living in the country of our ancestor's birth! And how fortunate that history repeated itself when Liz followed in our ancestor's footsteps, journeying from Germany to Key West, at just the right time!

*—Jeanne Brookman, Washington*

# The Benefits of Lost Luggage

$\mathcal{I}$ really got into family history after my mother died. She had often spoken with nostalgia about her roots in Vidlin, Shetland, off the northern coast of Scotland so I decided to visit this place, which sounded like the end of the earth to me.

Our trip got off to a rocky start when our luggage was lost by the airline. Grouchy and forced to wait at Lerwick airport while it caught up with us, I passed the time browsing a local tourist guide. I noticed a mention in the guide that the local family history society was meeting that evening. Well, why not? That seemed as good a starting point as any.

I attended the meeting and asked about my grandfather, Gilbert Sutherland. Someone produced a local history indicating that he was born at "the Pund." Then I went to Vidlin and asked the first person I met if this peculiar name meant anything to him. He kindly offered to take me there.

A mile or so down the road, he pointed to a derelict croft. I stood on the threshold of my grandfather's home, not much more than a shanty, and looked across the loch. It was totally quiet and very beautiful and must have been exactly as he had seen it. This moment became even more meaningful when I discovered later in my stay that my great-grandfather Robert had been born in this same spot in 1826 and lived there until his death in 1908. It awed me to ponder all the blustery, wet winters he had endured in this crude shelter of stone and thatch.

To stand where they had spent their whole lives and realize that the scene had remained unchanged for over 170 years was a deeply emotional experience. And much as I hate to admit it, the credit for the whole chain of events that had so effortlessly led me there belonged to my lost luggage. I'll think twice before complaining the next time!

—*Don Rutherford, United Kingdom*

*This is the Pund when it was a working farm.*

*The Pund as it is today—croft in center.*

# Mother's Last Gift

*M*y eighty-five-year-old mother passed away in May 1999. Shortly before, she emphatically told me that she wanted all eight of her siblings listed in her obituary. She wanted to make sure "her people" were recognized at the time of her death.

When making the arrangements for her funeral and obituary, I naturally wanted to carry out her final wishes. Others tried to talk me out of it, as they felt it wasn't necessary since Mom's siblings had all passed away many years ago; but I held my ground due to an overwhelming feeling that Mom had had some reason for being so adamant.

At the funeral parlor a tiny, elderly woman came to pay her respects. I did not recognize her, nor did she seem to know any of our family members. She clung to my hand and kept repeating, "My family didn't want me to come. They think it is so wrong of me to invade your grief."

After several minutes of apologizing, she introduced herself as Naomi and told me about the strong feelings that had convinced her to come that day. She had scanned the obituaries that morning, and seeing a reference to my mother's maiden name, went on to read it. The maiden name of Volz was the same as her grandmother's maiden name. When she saw the names of Mom's siblings, she was struck by how many of them were the same as the siblings of her grandmother.

Then Naomi pulled a paper out of her purse. It was a copy of a page from her family Bible with entries in Old German script. As she deciphered them, I learned that four of the fourteen children listed overlapped with the names of my mother's brothers. When she continued, I was stunned to hear the name of my own grand-father, along with that of his twin brother. Naomi's grandmother and my grandfather were brother and sister!

Naomi and I are delighted to have expanded our families. She has been doing genealogical research for twenty years. I have always had an interest, but our connection has given me the spark for research. Working together, we have begun to open new doors to our history in only a few short months.

I truly believe that bringing Naomi and me together was Mother's last gift. She instilled in me a love of family and history, and knew how important this connection would be to me. Both Naomi and I trusted our intuitions. Doing so has brought us new family, a connection with the past, and a legacy for my mother.

—*Faye Berra Venegoni, Missouri*

# Dancing Ghosts

*I* had made several trips to Chester County, Pennsylvania, in search of my ancestors. Through early maps, I had located the general vicinity where my great-great-great-grandfather Crisman had lived in the early 1800s. On one occasion, I had pulled over on a small road and mentally conjured up a house in the adjacent cornfield where he might have resided. Little did I know how close to the truth I was.

On my next trip a couple of years later, I took my teenage daughter. Granted, teenagers are rarely interested in family history, but she had been my good luck charm more than once and was to play a decisive role in what happened next. We returned to that same road and started at the far end where modern subdivisions had not yet invaded. My aim was to try to find the foundation of a house. We drove down several private lanes, looking at the houses and ultimately rejecting them because they were too modern or "didn't feel right." You see, I strongly believe ghosts tap you on the shoulder when you get near to the truth.

Feeling discouraged, we entered the last lane on the road. In a moment we saw an old fieldstone barn of German design, a small cottage, and a fieldstone house. As I knew my ancestor was of German heritage, I began to feel a distinctive pull toward the dwelling. Could it be? We went to see if anyone was home.

An elderly lady came to the door. I introduced myself and my daughter and explained our reason for being there. Mrs. Brown did her best to answer my questions about previous owners of her property. Within minutes, she had mentioned several names I had seen in the old deeds. Now the ghosts were dancing!

She invited us into the main room. It was spacious with a walk-in fireplace filled with nineteenth-century cooking implements. She told us she came to the house as a young woman when her father had bought and restored it. She and Mr. Brown had lived here for years.

After twenty-five years of research, I began to feel that I was possibly experiencing the greatest discovery of my "genealogical career." While I was effusing to Mr. Brown about his beautiful house, my daughter came running in from the front porch yelling, "Mom, Mom, this is it! Come see!" She led me out to where Mrs. Brown had pointed out the date plate over the front door, bearing the inscription:

C

J & J

1813

I knew then, without a doubt, that this was the home of my great-great-great-grandparents, James and Jane Crisman, built in the year 1813! There followed much excitement and picture-taking.

My eternal gratitude goes to the Browns for taking such good care of the house and, of course, the ghosts!

—*Chris Bell-Puckett, Ohio*

# Always Listen to Your Mother!

*U*nexpected connections are the greatest treasures. Mine came in a chance phone call to a cousin I had met years ago while I was in college.

Before she died, my mother, Thelma, the youngest child in a Lithuanian-Jewish immigrant clan, listed all her family members for me. By then, all the immigrants had died and their children had scattered. Thelma never understood what it is that drives genealogists, but she loved and guarded contact with friends and family, and it was her advice—to call friends and relatives whenever I went someplace they lived—that made the magic connection.

A decade after Thelma died, I decided to write the story of her family, starting in Waco, Texas, where the four Goldberg siblings and their spouses had settled, lived out their lives, and now rested in tiny Hebrew Rest Cemetery. I assumed I knew all I could ever learn about them because the first two generations had died. But something, probably Thelma's spirit, told me to call Polly, a cousin I had known briefly years earlier. Why her, I had no idea. I didn't even know if I could find her, but the voice said to try.

After some effort, I managed to locate Polly. What she told me revealed our shared past just as if she had opened the door to a room where all our extended family were gathered. The first woman in the family to attend college, she gave me a copy of her college biology project—a 1930s study of the immigrants, their spouses, and children. On a big sheet of butcher paper she had recorded all their names, vital statistics, marriages, children, personality quirks, talents, and work. It was a veritable time capsule!

With Polly's chart and the stories she told me, I tracked all four families down to the present and found four cousins, one descendant of each Goldberg immigrant, who gave me treasured bits of the family story. Within five years all four had died, but not before imparting their precious gifts of memory to me. Their contributions to the family story will live so long as anyone cares about this patch in the great American quilt. All because I heeded my mother's advice.

—*Linda Kilgore Zeigler, Texas*

# I Just Had to Go to Germany

*My* family had been researching a Bavarian branch for some time and kept running into brick walls. Finally, we had a breakthrough in the form of a naturalization record. This led us to a ship record that showed the family (including seven children) had come to the United States in 1845, but failed to give their town of origin.

We were stuck again until a genealogy professor suggested that some of the children might have been of the right age to fight in the Civil War. A check turned up pension records for two of the boys. In one of these pension files, a single affidavit revealed that the family had come from a town called Kronach. Now we knew our town of origin!

It was at this point that I felt compelled to go to Germany. Some may call it an inner voice, instinct, or gut feeling. I call it Spirit and decided to heed its call. This seemed a little excessive since I live close to Salt Lake City with its abundance of genealogical riches, but something kept telling me that it wouldn't be good enough to conduct this research from a distance. I just had to go to Germany.

My wife and I planned the trip and finally went two years later. Through a series of mishaps, we wound up with very little time in Germany, and our querying around Kronach for our family was turning up absolutely no leads. Now I was getting confused, because I was so sure there was a reason that I was meant to go there.

Finally, through a series of what I believe to have been Spirit-driven "chance" encounters, we found ourselves in a village about three kilometers from Kronach. There, we were quickly directed to the house of a man with the name we were seeking: Gaslein. In a strange twist of fate, the gentleman spoke excellent English, which he had learned after having been captured in World War II and working as a cotton picker in Texas. He was thrilled to meet us.

I showed him a descendancy chart and he insistently dragged me upstairs to an office where one wall was plastered with a huge chart showing the Gaslein family back to the 1400s. He then pulled out a file that turned out to be for my immigrant ancestor. After forty years of researching the family, our branch was the only gap in his records. After we exchanged more information, he led me to the small cemetery where our family was buried. Without his help, we would never have found it.

My wife and I returned home and told everyone our incredible story. The family was equally excited, so my mother decided to write a newsletter to share our tale with our extended clan. One of my cousins had a business trip to Germany coming up just a few months later and decided to go see for himself. When he got to the village, he was directed not to a house, but to the family cemetery. In it was a fresh grave belonging to the kind cousin who had given all the family history to me just a short time earlier.

We later learned that our genealogical benefactor had no surviving children. If we had not found him when we did, forty years of research—and the family history back to the 1400s—would have died with him. You can be sure that I will always listen to the guidance I receive from the Spirit.

—*Tim Powers, Utah*

# What Made Me Say That?

$\mathcal{A}$ few years ago I traveled to the Missouri Ozarks from California in search of the graves of my great-grandparents, Gilbert Williams and Sallie Simpson Williams. I knew they were buried in a private cemetery in the community of Greer, Missouri, but I didn't have a specific location.

I drove into the Greer area, but found no town there. As I saw no one to ask for directions, I stopped on the side of the road to decide what to do next. Just then, I spotted a car coming up a dirt lane near where I had parked, so I quickly jumped out and flagged it down. When the driver stopped, I asked if she could tell me where the old Williams farm was located. She pointed down the lane from which she'd just emerged and confirmed that the cemetery was also there.

Then for reasons unknown to me, I heard myself asking her if she'd ever heard of "Uncle Pete" Williams. He was one of Gilbert and Sally's eleven children and had died in 1948. Why I had chosen to ask about him in particular was a mystery to me.

She eyed me curiously. "Why yes," she said, "he saved my life when I was a baby." She explained that he was what was referred to as an "old-fashioned doctor" or "herb doctor," and he had used his faith-healing skills to cure her from thrush, a condition that attacks infants. He had been the postmaster at the time and her mother had taken her to the post office for treatment.

I had "accidentally" stopped at the lane leading to the very gravesite I was seeking and collected a wonderful story about my great-uncle who'd died shortly after I was born. I don't know what prompted me to stop in the right location or who prompted me to ask the right question, but I found far more than I was looking for.

—*Nona Williams, California*

# I Will Always Love You

$\mathscr{I}$ am relatively new at genealogy and have been researching for about five years. About three years ago, I was focusing on my mother-in-law's family, trying to find her grandparents. My mother-in-law's name was Areita Vivian Jones Sherburn. Mom had passed away in December 1992. At her funeral, the popular Whitney Houston rendition of the song "I Will Always Love You" was played. After that, it was very difficult for my husband to hear the song, until I told him that he would have to remember that whenever it came on the radio, this meant his mom was with us. Since then, hearing that song and knowing she is with us has always been very comforting.

Not much was known about my mother-in-law's grandparents, Charles and Sarah Jones. Some said they were from Pennsylvania, while others said they were from New York. Fortunately, I discovered that they were buried in a local cemetery, so I thought I would go over and see if I could find their gravestones.

As I drove through the cemetery gates, I realized how futile this undertaking would probably be—the cemetery was huge and Jones was such a common name. I continued on the drive and found myself in the old part of the cemetery. As I rounded a bend and saw yet another stretch of tombstones, I became even more discouraged. How would I ever find what I was looking for in this ocean of graves?

Not knowing what else to do, I decided to stop the car and get out and walk around. Just before I shut off the engine, I heard the first notes of "I Will Always Love You" come on the radio. The hair on the back of my neck stood straight up. I said, "OK, Mom, you're with me and going to help me on this one."

Before I got out of the car, I looked out the window to the left. Up on the hill about 50 feet away was a stone with the name Jones on it. I walked up to it and saw the names I was seeking: Charles and Sarah Jones. I knew then that Mom was truly with me.

—*Diana L. Sherburn, Michigan*

# A Prophetic Doodle

*I* first became interested in my family genealogy in 1966 at the age of seventeen while waiting for my father to pick me up from the library. My research progressed sporadically over the years as I was busy raising a family.

In 1978, I found myself doodling a landscape as I talked on the phone one day. In the landscape was a large tree—possibly oak or pecan—without leaves sitting in a field with low hills in the background and stones nearby. For some reason, this doodle struck me as important, so I put it in a scrapbook. After that, the doodling stopped.

Fourteen years later, in 1992, a man named Ronnie Brooks walked into the newspaper office where I work to place a classified ad. Ronnie and I chatted, and he mentioned his recent discovery of a gravestone for William Babb, a Revolutionary soldier, while he was out riding on his four-wheeler near his house. I immediately sensed this was the grave of one of my ancestors, the first William Babb who settled in Baldwin County, Georgia.

Ronnie gave me directions to the spot and a few days later on a cold December afternoon, I drove down the road. Imagine the overwhelming feeling I got when the picture I had doodled so many years before unfolded before my eyes. There sat the big pecan tree with the low hills in the background and granite boulders on the right. I drove up a little road and on my right on a little hill, sat a lone granite gravestone, weathered by nature. The gravestone, placed there in 1930 by the local chapter of the DAR, was surrounded by unmarked graves. I had found Grandpa after all these years—or did Grandpa find me?

—*Eileen Babb Sumner, Georgia*

# Meeting over Coffee

*T*wins run in my family, but I didn't know that until just recently. I had always known that my aunt and uncle—Gitte and John—were twins, but I thought they were the only ones. What I didn't know about were the twins my own mother, Inge, had given birth to.

My mother's story begins during a night on the town with several friends in her hometown of Holte, Denmark. Later that evening in 1938, she became a victim of rape but wasn't even aware of it since she had passed out. Three months later, troubled with unexplainable dizziness and vomiting, she went to a doctor and was given the startling news that she was pregnant.

Because an out-of-wedlock pregnancy would bring shame to her family, my mother was sent to another part of the country during her pregnancy. She had no choice about keeping the twin girls born of the attack. Societal pressure at the time and the whole episode surrounding their conception was too great, and she was forced to surrender them for adoption. She was at least allowed to give them their names—Lise and Inger—before they were taken from her in December 1938 when they were two weeks old.

For more than sixty years, the trauma of this rape has tugged at my mother, but far more distressing was the separation from her daughters. Every day since, she longed to see the girls. She wondered whether life had been kind to them, how they might look, had they married and had children of their own.

One of the conditions of the adoption was that my mother never contact the twins or try to find them. She broke that condition only once. After emigrating to the United States, she returned to Denmark in 1953 to search for the twins. With her sister Gitte's support and encouragement, she contacted the adoption agency, but they wouldn't give her any information.

Resolving to simply accept the situation, she never spoke about the twins. She did, however, share her secret with my father, Soren. When he proposed marriage, she felt it was appropriate that he should know.

The second time she shared her secret was just a couple of years ago when she and I were watching a television show about having twins. Catching me completely off-guard, she commented, "That's a lot easier than when I had twins."

In response to my total befuddlement, she told me what had happened. I immediately said that we had to find them, but she refused, saying she had signed a paper. She was also concerned about whether it would be good for the girls to find out, but was finally persuaded to look for them.

Finding the twins was likely to be difficult. My parents had left Denmark in 1948 to move to the United States and assumed that records of the twins' birth had been lost in the tumult of World War II. What we didn't know was that in Denmark, daughter Lise had discovered she was adopted only after her adoptive mother died in 1994, and had immediately set about finding her birth mother. A family member of Lise's was a genealogy buff and managed to trace her birth mother to a house in the Danish town of Holte, north of Copenhagen. He visited the house and was taking a photograph when the owner invited him in for coffee. Over steaming cups of java, he related the story of the twins and explained that he was searching for their birth mother.

Then last year, my uncle John, who had also emigrated to the United States, went to Denmark to visit his twin sister, Gitte. During this trip, John also returned to the family's hometown of Holte and visited the house where they all grew up. As he was standing outside, the homeowner came out and invited him in for coffee. John explained who he was and the homeowner gave him the telephone number of Lise's relative.

When Uncle John found out about Lise, he couldn't wait to share the news with Aunt Gitte so they could both call Mom back in the United States. But when he arrived at Gitte's house, he found that she had been taken to the hospital. She died a short while later.

Within hours of Gitte's tragic death, Lise was on the phone to Mom—her birth mother—in America. She called her "Mother Inge" in Danish and Mom was thrilled. It was something she had wanted all these years, and she was especially happy that the twins were just as excited as she was. For decades she had worried that perhaps they didn't want to see her because she had given them away.

Lise flew to the United States to meet her rediscovered mother. Mom and Lise looked at each other, embraced, and cried. She told us all about her own family, which includes her husband, Erik, and two children. And she was able to meet the rest of her American family, including two half brothers and two half sisters, many nieces and nephews, and her stepfather. The reunion will be complete when all of us return to Denmark to meet the other twin, Inger, who is afraid of flying.

"When you get a surprise like this, it gives you a new start to life," says my mother, now a young eighty-five. And we believe it was Gitte who gave us this incredible gift in her passing. On the very day we lost one loved one, two new loves came into our lives. We are certain it was Gitte who brought the twins back to us.

—*Kirsten Swenson, California, as told to Carole Rafferty*

PART TWO

# Connecting
# with Kin

*A*lthough genealogy is at its heart the study of long-deceased ancestors, connecting with living relatives has become almost as important to many family historians. Easy communication and ready access to ever-expanding resources have combined to provoke this development over the last decade.

Some seek living kin in an effort to track down family photos and documents. In whose hands might those treasures have landed? Trace your lines forward to the present and maybe you can find out. Others do it to find family history playmates—folks who are just as interested in your family as you because they *are* your family, even if your common ancestor lived three hundred years ago. Increasingly, people use genealogical techniques to track down relatives who have gone missing in just the last generation or two. Most recently, a few pioneers have begun exercising their family detective skills to save lives—to locate potential donors or warn of possible medical dangers. Whatever the motivation, one of the most addicting aspects of genealogy is the thrill of finding distant cousins, or in some cases, parents, children, or siblings.

Reunions—whether on-line, through the mail, or in person— are happy events that bring joy to all involved. If you've been fortunate enough to experience one yourself, you know that there is something about shared blood that overcomes separations caused by time, distance, or events. It's almost useless to try to explain it; one has to experience it to understand, but it's very real.

It doesn't matter that the common forebear lived in seventeenth-century France; there's still an instant feeling of connection. It doesn't matter that your relatives speak Slovak while you speak English; they're your family. It doesn't matter that your family was split by war, untimely death, or adoption; once the ties are rediscovered, it's as if the division never occurred.

These stories illustrate the power of genealogy to rebuild the severed bridges that have separated so many families for so many years.

# Ever Changing

*My* daughter and I had been searching for the origins of my grandfather, Alfred Denny, for several years. We had nothing definite except that he married Minerva Ann Hamilton in Michigan in 1860.

When I was a small child, my father had given me the address of his "Aunt Maggie," Mrs. William Rarick of Everson, Washington. She and I exchanged letters for about three years while I was still a youngster. My father died without giving any further information about his relatives.

About eighty-five years after my correspondence with Aunt Maggie, I decided to see if I could pick up the trail and find out exactly how she fit into the family puzzle. By then I was in my nineties so I knew the odds were not on my side, but I called the telephone operator for a number of anybody by the name of Rarick in the town of Everson, Washington. She told me they had a Charles Rarick and an L. Rarick. I asked her to ring Charles, but there was no answer so I asked her to try L. Rarick.

A woman answered and I said, "Hello, this is Carleton Denny. I'm trying to locate relatives of Margaret Rarick."

The lady on the telephone took a long breath and hesitantly said, "She was my grandmother."

I learned that Aunt Maggie was my grandfather's half sister. The "L" stood for Luella, who still used her maiden name. I had found my family!

What made this connection all the more remarkable, though, was that the operator had not heard me correctly. Instead of giving me the Raricks in Ever*son*, she had given me listings for Raricks in Ever*ett*, which was more than a hundred miles away from the town I thought I was calling. Checking later, I found out that there are no Raricks listed in Everson anymore. A lucky mistake, don't you think?

—*Carleton Denny, Arizona*

# A Class-ic Connection

$\mathscr{A}$s a way of getting my first-graders to write, I share my e-mail address with them. This year, I found myself corresponding with one little girl in particular—Gabrielle.

Recently, as part of my ongoing genealogical research, I sent a query to a family history mailing list seeking help. A short while later when I checked my mail, I saw Gabrielle's address and prepared to jot out a short note in return.

Instead, it was a message from Gabrielle's mother, telling me that she was responding to my recently broadcast genealogical plea, as she thought there was a possible connection between our families. We did some talking and sharing of information and ultimately discovered that we share ancestors eleven generations back in the 1600s—Joseph Loomis and Mary White, one of the founding families of Windsor, Connecticut.

The next school day, Gabrielle came up to me and told me that she had a secret to share. She whispered that she was my cousin, which, of course, I knew by that point. I asked her if we should share the news with the class and she said that she'd like to keep it our secret for a bit. About five minutes later she told me that it was time to tell *the news*.

I had talked about my research before, so the class knew what I meant when I mentioned my family tree. I told them that I had just found out that one of them was my cousin. The debate started as to which one of them it might be. Several were sure that it was them, but wondered how I knew. Gabrielle just sat there and didn't say a word.

I looked over at her and she nodded her head. I said, "Class, I'd like to introduce you to my cousin . . . Gabrielle." She beamed, and some of the children told her that she was lucky! One of them told me to keep looking for more people so that maybe she would be my cousin, also. Later that day, some children from the other first grade class "tattled" on Gabrielle, telling me that she was telling everyone that she was my cousin. They were quite chagrined when I told them it was true.

I guess I'm going to have to be careful now so I don't find myself accused of nepotism!

—*Deborah Hudolin, Illinois*

# Looking for Margaret

The last time Margaret and I were together, tiny partners in survival, she was eight and I was four. My sister and I were separated for more than six decades.

Our father divorced our mother in New York in 1929 and quickly remarried. Soon there were no kind words, no signs of love, no Christmas or birthday presents, nor even enough food. We often foraged for food when our parents were gone.

When our stepmother gave birth to her first child, our father gave Margaret away to another family without benefit of formal adoption. After neighbors complained to authorities about my neglect, I became a ward of the county and was sent to a series of foster homes. Separated by harsh circumstances, we soon lost touch.

Completely unknown to me, my sister worked, married, and raised a family. A husband and children were all she ever wanted, but she often told her family about her sad and lonely childhood.

On Christmas Day last year, Margaret's daughter Tina decided to try searching for her mother's lost brother on the Internet. She went to a well-known genealogical site and keyed in Margaret's maiden name. Up popped a message I had posted in which I mentioned a Margaret Felt with a birth date that matched her mother's, so Tina sent me a quick e-mail.

Christmas night in Seattle, my wife and I returned from a party and checked our messages. I let out a gasp as I read Tina's message that began "I've just returned from my mother's house and she told us of the brother from whom she was separated long ago . . ."

"Oh, my God, look at this," I called to my wife, afraid to believe I had finally found my long-lost sister. I had hunted for her for years, checking telephone directories wherever I traveled, revisiting our old neighborhoods in New York and New Jersey. I was even in the process of hiring a private investigator.

Both Tina and I were afraid a scam artist might be at work and hesitated to believe we'd solved the mystery. For a day or two, we exchanged messages, asking for more details. When Tina saw my home page entitled "Looking for Margaret," with photos of me at a younger age and apparently bearing a strong resemblance to her brother Tom, she called her mother.

Tina told her mother, "Mom, you better sit down, because I think I found Joe." Her mother sobbed. She couldn't talk.

On the other side of the country, I was also choked with emotion and asked my wife, Sunnie, to telephone my sister. Sunnie called and said, "I'm calling for Joe. He's crying and he can't talk."

A few weeks after the e-mails and phone calls, Sunnie and I flew to Tampa for a tearful reunion with my sister and her family. We hugged and bawled for at least fifteen minutes straight in the airport lobby while the rest of the family stood around us and cried too.

There was a lot of catching up to do. Margaret now hopes to meet our two half-sisters whom I've also located in my genealogical search, and I continue looking for information on our birth mother and ancestors in Hungary. I can take my time, though, because I've finally found Margaret!

—*Joe Felt, Washington, as told to Elizabeth Pope*

# More than Names on a Chart

$\mathcal{A}$cute myeloblastic leukemia—this devastating diagnosis was given to my twenty-seven-year-old daughter, Karyn Olson, in 1991. She needed a marrow transplant. Twenty-three years of genealogical research had given me the joys of meeting unknown relatives and making new friends. Now, my research records became a valuable resource in the search for a marrow donor. My files of charts, notes, and addresses formed the basis for a search to save her life.

A successful transplant requires the patient and donor to be tissue matched. The match is determined by serology, cellular, and DNA technology. Serology testing identifies antigens on the surface of white blood cells. Tissue typing is accomplished using blood samples to compare six antigens on an individual's genes. Everyone has two A, two B, and two DR antigens, having inherited one of each from their mother and the others from their father. At that time geneticists knew of 19 different A antigens, 40 different B antigens, and 15 DR antigens, all with many subtypes, which multiplied to thousands of possibilities. Genealogy enters the picture because a relative may have inherited the matching antigens.

Karyn's half brothers and half sister were not matches. We registered with the National Marrow Donor Program in an effort to find an unrelated donor. Due to the complexity of tissue matching, at that time only 20 percent of patients were able to find a donor. We also contacted donor banks in Canada and Europe. Months had passed and we were getting desperate.

Karyn's father is of 100 percent Swedish descent. Although Sweden had no marrow donor registry at that time, doctors at the

University of Uppsala Hospital agreed to type our Swedish relatives—cousins we had met through my genealogical research. Each test required a doctor's order and each time I was asked, "What is the exact relationship of this person to Karyn?" As time went by, I made many charts to show such relationships. Unfortunately, however, these Swedish lines did not carry the needed antigens. We turned to Swedish relatives in the United States.

Now it became apparent that the relatives most likely to match were descendants of my husband's maternal grandparents—the Johnson line. Again my genealogical charts came into use. At last a first cousin once removed provided a close, although not perfect, match. The search had taken eight months. The transplant took place. The new marrow generated nicely, but side effects from radiation and chemotherapy had left Karyn so weakened, she was not strong enough to survive the rigorous transplant procedure. Yet, her donor felt so positive about the experience that she arranged to be listed in the National Marrow Donor Program Registry.

My love of genealogy came close to saving the life of our beloved daughter, and it has the power to save others. It can heighten awareness of diseases that your family is prone to, or as in our case, help identify the distant kin with the necessary genetic characteristics for a vital transplant. Genealogy is more than a hobby; it can literally be a lifesaver.

—*Pamelia S. Olson, Washington*

*Comment about the National Marrow Donor Program:* Obviously the more donors in the pool, the greater the chance of finding that all-important match. This is one donor program where you can give the gift of life while you are still living. If you are called to be a donor, marrow will be harvested from your hips under anesthesia. The donor's marrow replenishes itself in six to eight weeks. For further information, please contact the National Marrow Donor Program at 1-800-MARROW2 (1-800-627-7692).

# A Fresh Branch

After the death of my grandfather, I got the genealogy bug. It started with the gathering of family photos and progressed to writing the family history. Several years ago, I took another step and began creating a Web site for Stovalls. During this initiative, I also pursued my Wallace, Cox, Raney, and other related family lines.

One day I received an e-mail about the Wallace line from a fellow named Ron Ritchie. Although I lived in Birmingham, Alabama, and he lived in Dallas, Texas, he had some Wallaces from the same area from which mine originated. We corresponded several times, after which he passed the baton to his daughter, Connie. She e-mailed me, and after six months or so, we reached the conclusion that we were not related.

With no more data to work on, we chatted about other interests and one thing led to another. The end result? This shy Alabama-born boy found himself flying to Dallas to meet a girl. During several subsequent trips, we explored the sights, met each other's families, and plotted our lives. In December of 1997, my genealogical penpal and I were married. Our search for roots had led instead to a fresh branch on our now combined family tree. I think it's only fair to give our ancestors the credit!

—*Tommy Stovall, Alabama*

# Lost Americans

*My* husband, Jim, and I were off to England after many years of planning, saving, and waiting for six children to be grown. In addition to the traditional sights, we were going to visit a small village, Shapwick. The only connection we had with Shapwick was that Jim's great-uncle lived there at the time of his death.

Driving from London, we were delighted to eventually turn off onto a quiet, winding country lane. As we crested the hill above Shapwick, a sunburst broke through the clouds to light the village of old stone cottages. Two large mansions anchored the village along its one main road. We quickly found the address of Uncle George and a few old-timers who actually remembered him, but could tell us little of his family.

At the center of the village stood St. Mary's Church, surrounded by gravestones—a fertile field indeed for genealogists. Jim headed for the front of the church, while I scouted the back. Within minutes we were both calling, "Come here!" Jim had found the headstone of his grandfather's parents, while I had found those of his grandmother's ancestors.

Perhaps, we thought, the church records might give us more clues. Some ladies referred us to the vicar, Reverend Baxter. Just as Shapwick fulfilled my dreams of an English village, so too did Reverend Baxter fulfill the role of English vicar. With a flowing beard, the seventy-something minister listened as we asked for a peek at the parish records. Our hopes were dampened when he said that only the current registry book was in the church, the older books having been sent to the main records office as they were completed. Nevertheless, we went to have a look.

I began to understand the difference between England and the United States better when the vicar told us that St. Mary's was built in the 1390s to replace the "old" church. The registry book was indeed "new" to St. Mary's, but the records went back as far as 1850! There we found the signatures of Jim's grandparents on their marriage record. Turning back pages we quickly found several additional generations of Godwins and Saunders.

From a vague quest to find one or two facts, we had discovered Jim's father's entire heritage. We wanted to attend a service at the church where many generations of his family had worshiped, so we asked about local accommodations. One of the original manor houses had become a hotel, where we quickly booked a room for the night.

We walked to St. Mary's on Sunday morning to join in the lovely Anglican service. At the close of the service, Reverend Baxter introduced us as American visitors searching for our roots among the Godwins and Saunders. As the last hymn faded away, a tiny lady grabbed us and said, "You've been lost for fifty years and now I've found you!" Within a few minutes, we unraveled her excitement enough to discover that Dora Watkins was a second cousin of Jim's.

We invited Dora to come to tea with us at the hotel to catch up on the missing fifty years. She quickly agreed, but had to go home to call her other cousins about our amazing appearance. At two o'clock, Jim went down to the great hall to wait for Dora while I finished dressing. Within minutes he burst back into our room yelling, "Dora's here!" I wasn't surprised since we had invited her and said so. Jim sputtered, "But you don't understand . . . she's brought the whole village with her!"

That might have been a slight overstatement, but Dora had indeed summoned Saunders cousins from near and far to meet the lost Americans. We spent a wonderful afternoon sharing photographs, letters, and family stories. The English cousins were much better at preserving things than we Americans, so we ended the afternoon with precious treasures of family history, but more important, with wonderful new friends.

—*Carol Godwin, North Carolina*

# Cherished

*C*elie was born on a dairy farm in southern Illinois during a severe snowstorm in January 1905. Her mother, Sophia, often complained about the cold, rain, and mud, and with good reason. She contracted tuberculosis and died just a year after her beautiful, dark-haired daughter was born. Celie was told that, due to the illness, her mother was not allowed to cuddle her tiny, three-pound baby girl.

After her mother's death, her father put her in an orphanage because, as she was always told, no one wanted her. Her father reclaimed her when he remarried, but seemed almost reluctant to do so. And her mother's family had apparently forgotten her existence as she never heard from them. Still, Celie comforted herself with the company of her half sister from her father's second marriage.

Celie married in 1927, and would have celebrated seventy years with her beloved Charlie, had he lived four months longer. After her half sister Gen passed away, Celie often complained to her children—including me—that she had no one left.

Reading some old family papers that were tucked away for years in a wooden box under my parents' bed, I felt an urge to visit Clarksville, Tennessee, where my grandmother Sophia's family had its roots. I asked my mother to come along. We drove to Clarksville and went to the library where we were told to contact a local historian. Bingo! The historian remembered my mother's grandparents because she had written an article about their business which was called "Dahlia Dell."

She explained that Dahlia Dell was the homeplace of a German family named Miller. There was a large spring on the place, a cemetery on a nearby hill, and a garden with dahlias of every size and color. The flowers were for sale along with other plants.

People drove by horse and buggy or walked out there on Sunday afternoons to look at them.

Inspired by this new knowledge, we were determined to explore Dahlia Dell and find the family cemetery. Locals warned us that the approach was not easy—that we would have to navigate a number of dirt roads and streams and the only clue of its former location was the Stables Restaurant.

For two days we drove around searching. Friendly folks directed us to many small cemeteries in the area, but we had no luck. Not willing to give up, I took one last turn into the parking lot of the Stables Restaurant before returning to Missouri. Suddenly, something compelled me to look up. Numb with excitement, I pointed to the top of the hill where we had looked many times before. There stood a lonely tombstone silhouetted by the sunset.

We scampered breathlessly through the weeds and briars up the hill. There was no question—this was it! My mother dropped to her knees crying and praying. I hugged the tombstone and yelled, "Thank you! Thank you!" And to my predecessors I gleefully exclaimed, "We've found you!"

The Miller cemetery had been excavated all around and looked like an apple core standing on its end. Seeing that it was in danger of being lost forever, someone had placed a new chain-link fence around it. I copied an Arkansas address from the small sign on the fence.

It took just a few phone calls to locate the man who had ordered it. He was one of my mother's first cousins! But even more astounding was the origin of his name. His name was Cecil and he had named his own daughter Cecilia. Both had been named for "Little Celie" of orphanage fame, for that was the last the family had known of her.

Through the years, my mother, Celie, was led to believe that her mother's family didn't want her, but she suddenly had proof that she was not only wanted, but cherished! People were named in her honor. She was dumbfounded. Nothing so wonderful had ever happened to her before. She was no longer the only one.

Cousin Cecil led her to his sisters and a brother. She visited and got to know her mother's people. For ten years the cousins showered her with love and affection until each of them passed away. They were a comfort to her when she was in her seventies and eighties.

My mother is now ninety-five. She says there is one last job to do. In one of the yellowed letters that was stored in the old box under the bed, she read that her mother, Sophia, was desperately lonely for her southern family before she died. Celie wants to see her mother brought home.

All by herself, Sophia lies in an unmarked grave in a cemetery in Illinois. I have promised my mother that I will gather some soil from Sophia's grave and symbolically take her to her beloved family—to the little cemetery in Dahlia Dell—where she too will be forever cherished.

—*Iola Allen Jasper, Missouri*

# Miss Universe

*I*sn't it funny how we all think of our grandparents as if they had no other role before *we* came into their lives? That's the way it was with me and Charlotte Wassef, my grandmother. I had always known that she was a little different from other grandmothers, but to me, she was always first and foremost Rhea's Grandma.

That rendition of her life crumbled one day when I was playing dress-up in her closet and Grandpa commented on how much I resembled her when she was crowned Miss Egypt. I realized then there was a lot I didn't know!

Grandma went into the closet and pulled out the traditional dress she had worn at the contest. It was inlaid with silver thread and weighed a ton when I tried it on my tiny frame. She told me that in addition to being the first Miss Egypt, she had also been crowned the first Miss Universe at the Brussels Expo in 1935! Grandma admitted that she had entered the contests against the wishes of her family; and because of her being from a minority in Egypt, there were those who resented her representing the nation. Yet with all this controversy, she had persevered, won both competitions, and become a representative

*Charlotte Wassef, Miss Egypt 1935.*

*1935 Miss Universe clipping from
great-grandfather's scrapbook.*

for women and an ambassador of peace, meeting with dignitaries all across Europe. Grandpa told me that her photo was used to sell beauty products all over the world and that she had even been offered an acting career in Hollywood, but turned it down to marry him.

When I was older, I realized not only how groundbreaking her choices were for that time and place but also, how painful it must have been for her, knowing her family disapproved. Curious to learn more, I pestered older relatives about our family history and was rewarded with a leatherbound scrapbook that my great-grandfather—Grandma's father—had put together.

Imagine my pleasure when I opened its pages to find that her disapproving father had carefully chronicled with photos and articles the successes of his rebel daughter! Even in the strict code of life in 1930s Egypt, he had been open enough to recognize his daughter's achievements for what they were. To this day, I admire Grandma's vibrant spirit, tenacious attitude, and ability to follow through with her convictions and find joy within the trials of life— qualities that have inspired me and that her father also celebrated in his own private way.

—*Rhea Alexander, New York*

# The French Connection

*N*ew to genealogical research, but armed with the research my sister Marie had already done, I began by searching through Catholic church records for Rochester, New York. My objective was to find children born in the mid-1800s to my great-great-grandfather, Jean Spacher, and his brother, Henry. In the baptismal records for St. Joseph's Church, I found the records I was seeking. They clearly noted the children's dates of birth and baptism, parents' names, and best yet, the place of origin for both parents!

I discovered through these records two different spellings: Farebersviller and Phaarebersweiler. We had always believed that the family came from Germany, but this village was in the Moselle region of France. Using church records for Farebersviller, I found still more records for my family. Ultimately, that church register in Rochester led me back through ten generations of Spachers, five in France and five in the United States.

Excited with my finds, I initiated contact with my French cousins. Last year, I went there for the first time to meet them. I traveled to Metz by train, where I had arranged to rent a car. My first surprise was when I was met at the station by half a dozen people—my cousins Erwin and Germain, their wives, and children. We exchanged greetings, dropped my bags at the hotel, and went to get my car. My trip nearly ended then because the agency had failed to tell me of a $1,000 deposit required of foreigners! Erwin, who had only known me for fifteen minutes, whipped out a credit card and told the rental

*American Greg Spacher, far right, with his French cousins,*
*including little Camille in front.*

agent that he would guarantee my rental. I could see I was
already family!

When I walked through the village of Haute Vigneulles, where
my sixth great-grandfather settled in 1690 and my fifth great-
grandfather was born, it became evident to me that I was
expected. Doors of the homes opened and people came out to
meet me as I walked. Repeatedly, I used my French to protest that
I wasn't that important, but this was always met with an insistence
that I was indeed very important because I was the first American
to return.

My cousins took me to other villages that had at one time been
home to my ancestors. In Bambiderstroff, I met another cousin,
Sebastien, who greeted us at the mayor's office. He brought out a
box of official-looking papers, and going through them one by
one, selected two and handed them to me, saying, "For you, so
that you will remember us, as we will never forget you." The documents were the original marriage contract for his great-grandparents and a contract of indebtedness between his grandfather and
his grandmother's family, documents I would never expect to see,
let alone be given.

Even I am surprised at how close I have become to my French cousins, and it moves me to see how much I have affected them. Before returning to the United States from this first trip, I spent the night in Metz because my train for Paris left very early, about 6 A.M. As I was sitting in my compartment waiting for the train to leave, we heard a commotion out on the platform. My compartment companion turned to me and said, "I think this might be for you." I looked out the window and saw about twenty people congregated there, all shouting my name and jumping up and down! My cousins had traveled the 30 kilometers from Haute Vigneulles to see me off! And then I saw Germain's daughter, Camille. She was waving and tears were streaming down her cheeks. I broke down and cried like a baby. I never expected the warmth and love that they shared with me, and it was then that I realized we really were family.

—*Greg Spacher, New York*

*Trans-Atlantic reunion—Spacher cousins from both sides of the ocean.*

# She Deserves to Know

*My* parents divorced when I was a baby and my mother kept me away from my dad. When I decided to trace my father's family, all I had to work with were my grandmother's vague memories. It was just last year that I received a copy of my own birth certificate and first learned my father's full name—Robert Leland Reed.

I received a copy of my father's death certificate on August 4, my birthday. It listed the executor of his estate as Diana Reed, who lived at the same address. I didn't know who Diana was, but decided to write her a letter, including pictures of myself and copies of birth certificates for myself, my father, and my grandmother. I included my phone number and a phone card, so there wouldn't be any reason not to call me.

Three days later, the phone rang and it was Diana, who revealed herself as my sister-in-law. She married my half brother, Randy, whom I had only met a few times as a child. Randy was my father's child from a previous marriage. She sadly informed me that my great-grandmother had passed away in 1985, my brother in 1996, and my father in 1997.

I started tearing up at this point in the conversation until Diana said, "And you have a four-year-old niece, Kimberly Allison." I almost fell to the floor! I talked to Kimberly for a few moments, and she called me "Aunt Michelle." Words cannot describe how I felt! I was laughing and crying all at the same time.

Diana told me that they had looked for me for more than fifteen years, but were unaware that my mother had moved out of state. When my father went in the hospital for the final time, Diana was the only one left to make his medical decisions. She told me that my family loved me and never gave up hope that they would find me or I would find them.

I plan on continuing my search for roots, more than ever. I want to know, and my little niece deserves to know.

—*Michelle Reed Whitnah, Arizona*

# Honeymoon Surprise

$\mathcal{I}$ began tracing my wife's Concilio family around 1990. Her one surviving aunt gave me some tidbits to get started—a few names and dates and a passing mention of their hometown in Italy. The following year, this ninety-three-year-old aunt died.

At the wake, one of the many cousins shared some information he had garnered from our aunt about a year earlier when he asked her about another Concilio family he had heard of in a town about 20 miles away. Out spilled a story that none of us had known.

She told our cousin that her father, Donato, had come to the United States in 1895 as a newlywed, and stayed for a brief time with his brother, Carmine. Donato and his bride soon moved a short distance away and set up a shoemaker shop. Relations between the two brothers and their families went smoothly for perhaps a quarter of a century, but sometime during this period, Donato loaned Carmine some money. Despite repeated attempts by Donato to elicit payment, Carmine never paid him back. Donato finally gave up and declared that he considered Carmine "dead." After that point, there was no further contact between the two families.

When I had quizzed our aunt about the family, all she said was that Donato had a brother and sister, and that his sister had remained in Italy, married a man named Luigi Landi, and had a daughter. Since she made no further mention of him, I just assumed that the brother had also stayed in Italy. Now I knew differently.

My interest in the family history proved contagious, as the cousin who shared this story also got the genealogy bug. He began by searching phone books in the local library and sending a form letter to those with the Concilio name. One of his first responses was from an Edith Concilio who turned out to be the last surviving child of our missing family! Had she married, we never would have found her.

During a visit with Edith, I gathered all the Carmine Concilio family information. She said that she always wondered why the visits from Donato's family stopped, but she was just a teenager at the time and not brought in on the family problems. I showed her my documentation of the family, and she showed me what she had, including several old letters from Italy. One was signed by a Concetta Landi. *Landi*. That name rang a bell! I instantly made the connection to Carmine and Donato's sister who had stayed behind in Italy.

The letter had an address in Italy, but what were the odds that there would still be a Landi family member in the house more than fifty years later? I wrote anyway and—wonder of wonders—the eighty-year-old granddaughter of Donato's sister replied! She was absolutely thrilled that contact with her American relatives had been reestablished after a break of half a century. We traded letters across the Atlantic—mine in English, hers in Italian—and I soon had this "new" branch documented.

Fast forward to 1995. One Sunday, I received a phone call in Italian-accented English from an airline employee in New York, asking if I could meet Concetta Landi at the Baltimore airport that Wednesday. I was flabbergasted and confused. Had my wife's eighty-five-year-old cousin impulsively hopped a plane for the States? "Oh no," the airline employee replied, "she's a young woman on her honeymoon with her husband." Apparently she was a niece of the other Concetta. Well, this was a surprise!

Of course, I agreed to pick up these spontaneous Italians. After all, they were our cousins! We made plans and hoped to spend a couple of hours with the young couple prior to what we assumed would be their honeymoon visit to Washington, D.C. during the cherry blossom season. I borrowed an Italian-English dictionary, and Concetta walked off the plane carrying one as well. I dropped words such as "rental car" and "hotel," assuming that they would get a car and follow me to our house for lunch before proceeding to their hotel in Washington. But I soon comprehended that *I* was the rental car—and the hotel!

Genealogy often brings families together, but sometimes in the most unexpected ways. In our case, it was a series of chance mentions and connections that culminated in my wife and me playing the completely unanticipated but pleasurable role of honeymoon hosts. Someday soon, we'll give our newfound relatives the chance to return the favor by guiding us around the old homestead in Italy. Maybe we'll even let them know we're coming!

—*Ken and Marie Kittelberger, Maryland*

# It Pays to Advertise

$\mathcal{O}$ur family went to a minor-league hockey game in Waco, Texas, about 90 miles from where we live. My son wore one of his favorite shirts, a jersey with his name in large letters on the back. About half an hour after we took our seats, a lady came down from the rows above us to ask if that was our name. She was curious because her family had the same name.

We eventually figured out that her husband, Ken, and my husband, Dennis, are indeed related. Ken's great-grandfather and Dennis's great-great-grandfather were brothers, making Ken and Dennis third cousins once removed. Neither family knew that the other branch even existed. Since then, we never pass up a chance to wear the family name. You never know where you might find new relatives!

—*Bobbie Stanfill, Texas*

# Probably Your Cousin

*N*on-genealogists tend to get spooked by the notion of "kissing cousins." Not in my family, they protest! But those of us who have been involved in family history for any length of time know that if you go back far enough, virtually every family tree sports a pair or two— or more. Even so, I wasn't quite prepared for what I found in the branches of my tree.

I began my research about three years ago. Because I grew up in Tennessee and my wife, Tina, was raised in Holland, Texas, where her family had lived for over a hundred years, I didn't expect to find any connections between our families.

Surprise! I discovered that Tina is my fifth cousin. Then I found out that my grandfather and grandmother on my father's side were ninth cousins. And then I learned that my Uncle Joe had unknowingly married his fourth cousin. And now it looks as if my parents might be ninth cousins. Connection after connection keeps popping up.

All of these newfound linkages give my poor, exhausted computer a run for its money in calculating relationships, and nowhere is that more evident than with my children. Jonathan and Victoria, besides being my children, are my fifth cousins once removed, my fifth cousins three times removed, my eleventh cousins once removed, and my eleventh cousins three times removed. They are the sixth cousins once removed, seventh cousins once removed, and twelfth cousins of their mother. And of course, they are also their own—and each other's— sixth cousins, sixth cousins twice removed, eighth cousins, twelfth cousins, and twelfth cousins twice removed! Phew!

You, the reader, are a complete stranger to me, but don't be surprised if someday down the road, you and I discover that we're cousins!

—*Matthew Van Hook, Texas*

*Comment:* This kind of conundrum is quite common in genealogy and can be a lot of fun to unravel. If you're like most of us and can't keep all these complex relationships straight (what exactly is a twelfth cousin twice removed anyway?), have a look at Lois Horowitz's *Dozens of Cousins* (Ten Speed Press, Berkeley, California, 1999), which does a great job making sense out of all this confusion.

# A Strong Hold

*In* 1867, shortly after the Civil War, Henry Strong of Brookhaven, Mississippi, emigrated to São Paulo, Brazil, along with his daughter, Sally Strong, and other Southerners. My branch of the family has remained in Brazil until this day.

About a year ago, my sister and I were searching for material for a biography of our grandmother and came across a little suitcase with letters written more than 130 years ago to our great-great-aunt Sally Strong by Tom Atkins, a Mississippian who was very much in love with her. In his letters, he made no attempt to hide his pain at her departure for Brazil: *"It will require a deeper stream than the Jordan of Death to wipe out the remembrance of my love for you . . . I will never marry in this Country while I know you to be alive and single . . ."*

Tom must have had quite a hold on Sally's heart as well, for she never married.

Just about the same time we discovered these letters, the Fraternity of American Descendants in São Paulo received an inquiry from an American, Janett Gibbs of Georgia, asking for information about the fraternity's annual reunion, since she knew some of her ancestors had emigrated to Brazil.

One day while I was conducting more research at the fraternity, I happened to tell an acquaintance about my recent suitcase discovery. Our discussion reminded her of Janett's letter, which she handed to me since I was one of the few English-speakers. Skimming through

*Tom Atkins proclaims his love for Sally Strong.*

its pages, I was stunned to see that the writer was inquiring about the Strong name, because she was apparently descended from a brother of Henry Strong!

I quickly unraveled that Janett and I were sixth cousins. How unexpected to suddenly come across a cousin this way! Janett and I corresponded, and she was able to add considerably to my knowledge of the Strong family. Among the papers she sent was a newspaper article from 1981 with a picture of the house built by Henry Strong in Brookhaven around 1857! I was fascinated to see my great-great-grandfather's house in America because the one he built upon arrival in Brazil had disappeared long ago amidst a sugar cane plantation.

Earlier this year, Janett came to the fraternity reunion in Brazil. A month later, I returned the visit and went to Georgia. Together we embarked on a road trip covering 1,730 miles in eight days! We visited cousins and searched for the Strong-Hill Cemetery. At the abandoned cemetery, we found the tomb of Henry's wife, who had not lived to emigrate with her family to Brazil. We also found the tomb of John Strong, Henry's father and the common ancestor of Janett and myself.

But the most magical experience was wandering the halls of the old Strong house that had so captured my imagination. Faye, the restorer, allowed us to explore, and Natalie, the owner, invited us to return during a planned reunion to tell the story of Tom Atkins and Sally Strong! This house, built by Sally's father, is one of the oldest antebellum constructions in that area and marks the spot where Tom and Sally met for the last time before she left for Brazil. Standing there, it didn't take much imagination to picture their wrenching farewell.

How strange that a suitcase in Brazil should contain the secrets of a house in Mississippi, and that the two should be relinked 130 years later through a "chance" connection of two virtual strangers. And how blessed I am to find new relatives, a rich history, and deep roots which, only a year ago, I knew nothing of.

—*Maria E. B. Byington, Brazil*

☙ *Comment:* For information about a forthcoming book on this story, contact Ms. Byington at meb@tecepe.com.br

# The Perils of Genealogy

$\mathcal{I}$, being the typical starry-eyed genealogist, began my search for my illustrious ancestors with a great deal of pride and anticipation. After all, generations of my mother's family had passed on the wonderful story of Elizabeth "Betsy" Ross, the flag maker, who was our ancestor. Oh yes, and on my father's side of the family, we had Wild Bill Cody, the famous buffalo hunter. My buttons popped off my chest every time I entered a library or courthouse.

Slowly, as I got deeper into my research, a dreadful, inescapable fact began to loom on the horizon. It became apparent that Betsy Ross had married a John Ross, but after only three years of marriage—and with not one single child born—he managed to get himself killed when a munitions storage building blew up! And with him went our claim to dear ole great-great-grandmother Betsy Ross.

Though a mite discouraged, I brightened up with the thought that we still had the shining star, Wild Bill Cody. But shortly after a trip to Clayton Library in Houston, my tail feathers began to really droop. I discovered that William Cody's father and mother had a totally different name than what *our* family lore had given to them. Tim-*ber*! There went another branch.

But I still wasn't done wreaking havoc on the family tree. My next contribution was the discovery that my great-grandfather was a deserter from the Confederate Army.

My family thinks that I went on some kind of kamikaze mission to destroy the family's name.

If I keep this up, the next branch that gets severed from the family tree might be my own!

—*Dee Guinn, Texas*

# The Brother
# She Never Knew

*T*wo years ago I was helping guide a heritage tour of Slovakia. One morning in Presov, I left the hotel and saw a woman from the tour standing with a small cluster of people near the entrance to the lobby. She was crying. I wanted to ask her what was wrong, but sensed that this was not the right time.

I saw her again later that day talking happily with the same people I had seen her with in the morning. This piqued my curiosity, but I was so busy that I couldn't stop to ask questions. The next morning we continued on our tour. She was sitting by herself in one of the window seats in the bus. I sat next to her and asked what I wanted to the day before, "Is everything OK?" She smiled and told me her story.

Six months ago she didn't have a clue about her Slovak relatives. She knew that her father had moved to the United States from then-Czechoslovakia, but he never discussed his past. When he died, she started doing some research and managed to locate the village of her father's birth. She sent a letter to the mayor of the village, but the reply came from a man sharing her surname. He wrote that his father had emigrated to the United States, but when his mother had refused to join his father overseas, the marriage ended. He never knew what had happened to him. Could they be brother and sister?

She continued, "At first we didn't want to believe that someone in our family would do something like this, but when we shared photos, there was no doubt that the person in both of our pictures was the same man—*our* father." So the person I had seen her crying with was her newly discovered brother.

I asked how she felt after uncovering this secret about her father's life. She smiled again and told me, "You know, I don't feel bad about it. There were many cases like that. But I'm happy that my father didn't leave them without being sure he looked after them from a material point of view, and only after his wife had told him she would not go with him to the States. They built a big house from the money he sent."

I felt privileged to have witnessed this sibling reunion, but there's more to the story that demonstrates how history repeats itself. This woman mentioned that when she found her brother, they shared all sorts of information about their families. Her brother told her that they had one more brother who moved from Czechoslovakia to Australia during the Prague Spring of 1968, but that he had broken off all contact with his Slovak family and no one had heard of him since. When I learned that there was another brother in Australia, I contacted some organizations there to help me find him, and sure enough, they found him. I will meet him in a few months and hope to be a small part of another reunion.

—*Martin Hyross, Slovakia*

# Is That You, Robbie?

$\mathscr{I}$n the summer of 1986 my husband and I decided to research my dad's family line in Louisiana. I had not researched his line since he and my mom had divorced when I was seven, and he died when I was not yet twenty.

Driving from Idaho, we arrived in Many, Louisiana, about dusk and decided to find a hotel before going to the cemetery where I knew he was buried. I had an overwhelming feeling I should stop at a particular hotel and my husband humored me. We went in and the lady behind the desk glanced up and then quickly back down at her paperwork. "Hi, Sue," she said, "I'll be with you in a moment."

When she looked up again, I corrected her, telling her that my name isn't Sue, but Robin. She stood there a second and said, "I could swear you were Sue Moore." I didn't know anyone by that name and went ahead and registered. Polite conversation ensued and she asked why we were in Louisiana. I explained that we were there to research my family and find my grandmother's grave.

She replied, "I'm from here. Who was your grandmother?" When I told her that her name was Edna May Rivers Moore, her response about knocked me over. "Edna May's not dead. She lives in Vidor."

Vidor was about two hours away in Texas. Since I hadn't seen her in about twelve years, I decided to try and contact her before leaving Louisiana. My husband and I then went to our room.

Two hours later there was a knock. There standing in the door was my grandmother and two ladies I didn't know. One looked so much like my little sister, I just stared. Grandmother said, "Is that you, Robbie?" This was the nickname she and my daddy had called me when I was little, and I hadn't heard it for years. She and I hugged and laughed and hugged some more.

One of the women with her was Sue Moore, the woman the desk clerk had mistaken me for. It was easy to see why because we were first cousins and had a strong resemblance. The other woman was another cousin.

I learned a lot about my daddy and his family. We went to the graveyard the next day, and saw Daddy and Grandpa's graves. We thoroughly enjoyed our unexpected reunion and I was very sorry when it was time to leave.

After our meeting, we talked a few times on the phone. Later that year on December 12, I had a strong feeling to call my grandmother, who turned out to be in the hospital. I called her and she was obviously happy to hear from me again. We talked for a few minutes and because she was tired, I told her good-bye. Two days later, she died. Although I was sad to lose her, I was so grateful to have found her just months before she passed away. Serendipity, just plain luck, or the guidance of the Holy Spirit. Call it what you want, but it does happen.

—*Robin Tyree, Oklahoma*

# Revitalizing
# the Family Tree

*My* adventure began four years ago in an ethnic enclave in Chicago and led me to a village on the Dalmatian coast of Croatia with a side trip to Yale University for lifesaving surgery.

I became involved in genealogy in the early 1990s and worked diligently on compiling a history of my maternal side, but it never occurred to me to include any paternal information. My father and his family had played only a minor role in my life since he died suddenly in 1956 at age thirty-nine, when I was six years old. At the time my mother was told that he had a rare illness that caused the cerebral hemorrhage that killed him. She thought it was called "Weber's Disease."

I traveled through several states learning all I could about my mother's family. During one of my many trips to the National Archives in Chicago, I impulsively decided to see if there was any information about my Croatian grandfather who had lived with us until my father's death.

I knew Djeda, as we called my grandfather, came from Croatia, but didn't know if he had ever become a U.S. citizen. In a matter of minutes, I found a reference to his naturalization. A few days later, I had a copy of the record in my hands. From it I learned the name of the village of his birth. After that, everything fell into place like clockwork, as if it were meant to be. Within three months, I made contact with relatives in Croatia and soon after started making plans to visit them. We were warmly received by our Croatian relatives, and by the time we left, we were very much a part of the family. Now all of my attention was focused on my father's family. I made contact with his American relatives and rekindled long-lost relationships.

By this time I knew that the family here suspected that there was a connection between the early sudden deaths of my father and his mother, but never knew exactly what the connection was. At the insistence of a dear friend, I finally agreed to try to find out something about the illness that killed my father. I remembered that in a "treasure box" I had for many years, there was a letter from a doctor. I don't know how I came into possession of the letter, but I knew it was there. I dug it out and learned the real name of the illness that I had long called Weber's Disease.

I got on the Internet and began searching for information about this illness. Part of me wanted to know more, but part of me preferred to remain blissfully ignorant. Suddenly, there it was: Osler-Weber-Rendu, now known as HHT or Hereditary Hemorrhagic Telangiectasia.

It took me all of five minutes to realize that I certainly had this illness. That was bad enough, but it was also clear that I wasn't the only member of my family who had it. Several of us had all the symptoms.

Thanks to the Internet, I discovered the HHT Foundation International. I soon learned that there were no doctors in Chicago who treated this rare illness. The good news was that the Yale University Vascular Malformation Center had doctors who specialized in and treated this condition. We would have to wait for six weeks for appointments to go to Yale for a screening. Once I had secured the appointments, I broke the news to my family.

Just as I suspected, we were all victims. I was in the worst shape and learned I had already suffered a stroke and had dangerously large vascular malformations in my lungs. I knew by this time that my grandmother had brought this hereditary illness from Croatia. She had died suddenly of a pulmonary hemorrhage at age forty-four and my dad had died at thirty-nine. I was already forty-six and living on borrowed time. So instead of my planned Christmas in Croatia, I was at Yale, undergoing a two-day procedure that gave me a new lease on life.

On my previous trip to Croatia I had only met my grandfather's family, but I knew now that I'd better start looking into my grandmother's side. Surely others in her line had this illness. My family in Croatia was so disappointed that I couldn't make Christmas that I was forced to confide my condition to one relative. The secret didn't last long. I promised to return to Croatia as soon as possible and I kept that promise. Six weeks after surgery I was on my way to Croatia, determined to trace the line and find the trail of the illness.

After learning I had the illness, I began corresponding with the Minister of Health in Zagreb, Croatia. He kindly accepted and distributed informational packets I had put together regarding the diagnosis and treatment of HHT. Those of us with the illness are obligated to educate others, especially our doctors and dentists, because a simple tooth extraction can be fatal.

I found the line of the illness and discovered that early, sudden death was a pattern. We can only guess how many lives have already been saved in our extended family, and how many more will be saved as we get the word out. I believe that there was truly a guiding hand in all of this, but never figured out just whose hand it was. I suspect it is the grandmother I never knew, whose bloodline and illness I share. I could have easily died young, but was instead left here for this purpose.

—*Nancy Andjelich Margraff, Illinois*

# PART THREE

# If at First You Don't Succeed . . . ◆ ◆ ◆

*W*hat's the most extreme tactic you've ever used in pursuit of your roots? Have you ever launched a mail campaign or searched through thousands of pages of microfilm? Perhaps you've traveled across the country to look at records for yourself after you received a negative response from an archive or courthouse. If you're a hard-core genealogist, you undoubtedly have a couple of war stories of how you've overcome some seemingly insurmountable brick walls in your research.

No one can ever accuse genealogists of lacking creativity and persistence in their heritage quest. Yes, it's true that the clues that build a family tree may be sprinkled around the world and there's no guarantee that they even exist. Deceptive clues may lead to false trails and years of fruitless research. But genealogical sleuths don't let minor details like this get in their way. It may take a while, but in the end, their determination and ingenuity ensure that they always "get their man." Here's hoping that the following stories spark an idea or two for tackling some of your own brick walls.

# Genetealogy

$\mathcal{B}$ased on an old story, I had always believed that my Savin family had originally come from France. In 1938 when my father and his parents were on holiday, they met another family called Savin. Meeting a family with the same unusual surname was extraordinary enough, but they also knew the family's origin. They told of a French Huguenot family who escaped to England in the seventeenth century.

In 1986 I came across a book about surnames, but was not convinced that this book had investigated our surname properly. I began to collect any reference to Savin I could find. In an old copy of *Who's Who*, I found a Dr. Savin, seemingly the same Dr. Savin from before the war. I phoned his number, but found he had died.

I then decided to write to Savins in the U.K. phone book. Another Dr. Savin told the same Huguenot story and put me in touch with his aunt Annie, who turned out to be the sister of prewar Dr. Savin. This belief in their Huguenot ancestry was so strong that when Annie's great-niece was christened, it was conducted in one of the few Huguenot chapels left in England, and I was invited. The two Savin families who had met in 1938 met once again in 1994.

However, I was having my doubts as I was finding the Savin name in England centuries before the Huguenots came. Over the years, I unearthed evidence of still other Savin families and I wondered if they were all connected in the past. It was like having a jigsaw puzzle with missing pieces.

Then two years ago, I read an article about DNA proving the tradition that nearly all Jewish priests were descended from Aaron, brother of the biblical Moses. This gave me the idea that perhaps the various Savin families could be connected. I phoned one of the scientists at a university and, in all innocence, said I was thinking about doing similar research. He asked me about my technical background, qualifications, and institution. When I said none, there was a pause at the other end! He then suggested that I put my proposals in writing.

I waited and waited and heard nothing. Finally, I called and was told that the scientist I had spoken to was out of the country. However, the situation was explained to a Dr. Thomas. I traveled to London to meet Dr. Thomas, unsure if my proposal had been accepted or not. It appeared that they liked my idea, so the project finally started.

But now my task really began—to get as many DNA samples from Savins as I could. I wrote several hundred letters to male Savins on the British voters roll. Most did not reply, but about seventy did. To these I sent a simple DNA collection kit. Now came the task of tracing their Savin lineages.

The stationery, postage, travel, and certificate costs were mounting to many hundreds of pounds, so sponsorship was sought. I wrote to a genealogical institute. After a year of meetings and discussions, a check arrived.

At the university a few DNA results were produced, but then I had to be patient again. There was a processing backlog: mine was only one of forty projects. Months went by until finally, the results were available. Was the project going to prove anything after all this effort?

By genealogical methods, the participants were narrowed down to seven Savin family trees. But the genetics confirmed that three trees were in fact branches of the same tree, representing 65 percent of the candidates. I was part of this group. It also revealed that another three trees were very closely related and that one small tree was on its own.

As the definitive genealogical evidence could only take us back to the 1600–1700 time frame, the genetic research told us more than years of study of available documents could have even proved. Moreover, knowing which lines are ultimately linked with each other provides guidance for future genealogical research. The Savins unknowingly possessed the missing pieces to their family history puzzle. It was there all along, hidden in their DNA.

—*Alan Savin, United Kingdom*

# Ask and You
# Shall Receive

*W*hile researching my eighteenth-and nineteenth-century Masterson ancestors, my husband, Larry, and I wandered into the Brown County Historical Society in Georgetown, Ohio. There, we were greeted with the oft-heard "the courthouse burned" tale that genealogists so dread. That was our cue to go home frustrated, bemoaning our luck.

But positive as we are, we said, "OK, but what happened to the records?" The archivist looked surprised and said that no one had ever asked that question. She told us that the damaged records had been preserved—burned edges and all—and were located in a warehouse a few blocks away.

When we asked how we could search those records, she gave us a key to the warehouse! Hours later, covered in soot, we returned victorious to the historical society, having found the proof we sought between the covers of blistered books with charred edges.

Something told us that a burned courthouse doesn't necessarily have to mean the records have been destroyed as well. We asked. We received!

*—Reba Shepard, Florida*

# Righting Old Wrongs

*E*arly in my research, I obtained my great-grandfather's Civil War military service and pension records. They were a wonderful find and there was much in the way of previously unknown family information in them.

Because he indicated that he had married in Montpelier, Vermont, after the war and the file also included the date and minister's name, I decided to write to both the state of Vermont and the town clerk's office in Montpelier for a copy of the marriage certificate. After a long wait, a notice arrived from both agencies stating there was no such marriage.

At this point, I appealed to my wife to join me on a trip to Montpelier to make a personal visit to the clerk's office. Upon arrival at the town hall, we found the clerk, introduced ourselves, and mentally prepared for what I thought would be a "bad time." Instead, she was very congenial, expressed her disappointment at the negative results, and reassured me that there was no record of this marriage. She even offered to allow my wife and me to search through the card files and convince ourselves. We accepted this invitation and she showed us to a room containing many files recorded on index cards.

As I stood in this room, confident of the information in the pension file, something came over me that I can't quite explain. I asked my wife to look in the records under Riker, my great-grandfather's last name, as the clerk had done twice before, just to confirm her findings. Meanwhile, I was directed for some unknown reason to search for Brownell, my great-grandfather's *middle* name. What made me do this still puzzles me today.

There in the files was a card for the marriage between "James Brownell of Riker, New York" and Lauraette Demeritt. The date and minister's name matched those in my great-grandfather's pension records exactly. Apparently, the person recording the marriage back in 1866 had made an error that remained uncorrected for well over one hundred years.

We shared our discovery with the clerk and asked how to correct the error. She advised that we would have to appear before a probate judge with all the paperwork and have a ruling made on the case. What a wonderful feeling of righting an old wrong came over me as I strode into the probate court office to make an appointment to see a judge the next day. We stayed in a local hotel and used the time to prepare the affidavit to correct the records. The next morning we sat before Judge Nora E. Olich who, after considering the case, asked me one question: "Why are you bothering to do this, Mr. Verney, after all these years?"

I answered, "Your Honor, I was rebuked twice in my attempt to obtain copies of this record, knowing full well it must exist. Something told me to come here, and as if I were destined to, I found the error. By correcting it, I can ensure that no future family member will be denied copies of these records. Now my great-grandparents can rest in peace and I can go on with my genealogy research."

The judge thanked me and I paid the fee. I have in my possession both the erroneous and corrected copies as a reminder that persistence is its own reward.

—*Bob Verney Sr., New Jersey*

# Pots and Clans

"*There* were *no potters* in our family!" my uncle said emphatically. I had told him that his grandmother's death certificate said her father was William Neiffer, and I had reason to believe he was a potter in Pennsylvania. "Nope, *no* potters in the family!"

For a long time I had wanted to learn to cook in the fireplace. The solution presented itself when I arranged to be taught in exchange for becoming a docent at the restored colonial-era home in the next town. I was fascinated with the accouterments of the hearth, and in all the jumble of rough-hewn equipment, I frequently found myself running my hands over the glass-smooth glazed redware pieces. I bought a book to learn more about redware and came across the name of a Pennsylvania potter, William G. Neiffer, who had a pottery right about where I knew my grandmother had been born. The years in which he operated the pottery coincided with the years my ancestors lived. I had to explore further.

*Pennsylvania potter, William G. Neiffer.*

I wrote to the author, who directed me to the tax office where she had done her research, but it held no genealogical clues for me. Still, I just knew this had to be my great-

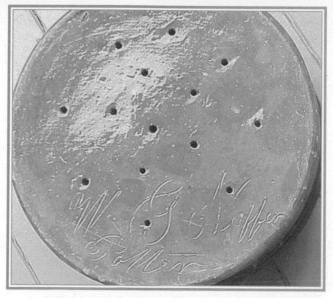

*Redware crafted and signed by William G. Neiffer.*

great-grandfather! It must be that my uncle had never heard because the information was lost over time.

I settled down to eat breakfast a few weeks later and grabbed a magazine from the top of one of my many piles. This one was an older issue of an antiques magazine devoted to folk art. It had been in my home for three or four years, but I had not yet read it. I crunched the first spoonful of cereal and began choking when I inhaled some of it as I read. There in front of me was a picture of a beautiful redware lidded colander signed by "W. G. Neiffer/ Potter"!

I recognized the name of the man who owned the piece, as he himself is a contemporary redware potter, and I called him excitedly to ask what he knew about the piece. He told me everything he knew of the colander's origins and invited me to his house to see it.

I wouldn't go to see it, though, until I had proof that it was made by my great-great-grandfather. I searched the census records doggedly for three more years. From tax records, I knew where William was living in 1860, that he had a wife with the unusual name of Vietta, and that my great-grandmother, Eliza, would have been two years old at the time. The census records were nowhere to be found.

Hours into the third vacation trip to the library, I sat in a glum slump in a quiet corner and tried to figure out why I couldn't find this clan. I tried to place myself in 1860 and slowly formed an idea that my ancestors, who were German, were probably giving their responses to an English-speaking census taker. How would the census taker deal with their names? How would he spell "Neiffer"? Perhaps he had written "Nifer" or "Niffer" or—wait a minute!—maybe "Knifer" as in "knife."

I marched back to the index again and was momentarily excited to see an entry for a William Knifer. I went a little more enthusiastically to the drawer with the census films—to the microfilm reader—to the page—to "William Knifer, age 25, occupation: master potter" with his wife, Fietta, age twenty-five, and his two-year-old daughter, Eliza Romalda. Yes! My grandmother had a niece named Romalda!

*Yes!* We *did* have a potter in the family, and he signed a piece of pottery, and someone found that signed piece half-buried in the dirt of a basement, and someone I knew bought it, and someone else published it in an old magazine that I bought years ago at my favorite used-book store in another state! And all of that had led me back to him.

*Now* I allowed myself to make the pilgrimage to see the large colander. I slowly traced my fingers over the signature of "W. G. Neiffer/Potter"—my great-great-grandfather and I, reaching out and touching each other almost a century and a half later.

—*Lynne K. Ranieri, New Jersey*

# A 4,000 Year
# Family Tradition

$\mathcal{I}$ remember as a little girl of six or seven in my native China seeing a book with a red cover. My father reverently told me that the book recorded the names of our Tseng ancestors and that we should handle it with great care.

I kept that memory with me when I left China in 1949. Because of events in China, it was difficult to even communicate with my family for many years, but in 1979, I was finally able to visit my mother and brothers and sisters for two weeks. There were so many life experiences to share with each other, and we shed many tears of both happiness and sadness. During this journey, I also hoped to see the red book my father had shown me, but was very disappointed when my mother told me that it had been destroyed during the Cultural Revolution in the 1960s.

Two years later in 1981, I returned to China to celebrate my mother's eightieth birthday. At the banquet, I asked my siblings if any of them could help me find the record. I knew what my mother had told me, but wasn't willing to accept defeat quite so easily. My younger brother Shao-qiang agreed to go to Jiang-Xi province where our grandfather had lived and ask around.

In 1982 he wrote that there was in fact a distant cousin named Chi-ng in a neighboring village who owned a set of ancient records. As I was about to learn, the fact that they still existed was remarkable.

Early in the 1920s when Chi-ng's father was dying, he handed nine thick books to his illiterate son and told him to guard them with his life. These were days of civil war and unrest, and Chi-ng was a humble farmer with no family. What could he do with this incredible responsibility?

In those times, every Chinese home had a variety of clay pots. They were used as rice and well-water containers, and for preserving meats, vegetables, and eggs. Chi-ng decided to put the nine books into a clay pot, cover them with small stones for pressure, and bury the whole thing beneath his bed under the ground in his humble house.

Some years later, a fire raced through the whole village and burned it to the ground. People rebuilt their homes in the same places where their old houses had stood. Then in the 1960s, the Red Guards searched out and destroyed thousands of cultural items all over China, including this village. But both times, this set of books remained hidden deeply underground, protected by layers of mud and dust. Their very survival was a miracle.

In winter 1982, Shao-qiang visited Chi-ng and asked if he could have a look at the books. Chi-ng told my brother that he would bring the books after Shao-qiang prepared a three-day feast. My brother did as he was bid and Chi-ng kept his end of the bargain. He arrived at the gala riding high on a tractor with a large package covered with a red cloth. A band of Chinese musicians led the way and a group of villagers followed. The whole group enjoyed eating and drinking for three days and nights. At the end of the third evening, my brother was finally permitted to lift the red cloth and hold the nine books in his hands for the first time. They were indeed the Tseng clan compiled genealogical records. He quickly glanced through them and copied twelve generations of names and dates of our father's direct line upstream. A short while later, he transferred the names to a pedigree chart and sent it to me.

I jumped with joy when I saw it, but knew that our job was not yet finished. I wrote back to my brother saying that I wanted a photocopy of that set of records, no matter what the price. Shao-qiang is a persistent fellow, so in 1983, he invited Chi-ng for a three-day visit. He also invited several escorts to ensure the protection of the books and promised them each a watch and help with starting a business back in their home village. They finally handed over the books and let Shao-qiang photocopy them.

But our endeavor was not yet over. We were not sure whether it was permissible to send the photocopied books to Singapore, where I was then living. Shao-qiang airmailed the first book and I received it safely! Then he sent the second, third, and fourth, and all arrived as scheduled! Just when we were becoming confident, though, we hit a snag when my brother sea-mailed the fifth and sixth together. They were stopped and returned at Customs with the explanation that they were not allowed out of the country. At the time Shao-qiang could not leave China and I was recuperating from surgery and could not travel. I had four books and he had the other five.

What to do? Slowly, through a two-year process of sending a few pages at a time in airmail letters, I finally assembled a complete set in 1985, by which time I had moved to Canada. It was so much effort for my brother to go through, but how priceless the result! The records contain *172 generations* of thousands of names with detailed dates and places. They go back to 1950 B.C. and include insights such as the fact that Confucius was very fond of one of my ancestors, Tsan. Many know that Confucius wrote five books as standard works for Chinese culture. It was our ancestor Tsan who wrote the sixth book on honoring one's parents and ancestors. This revelation made it clear that my brother and I had done the right thing. I am humbled that we were able to serve as an instrument in carrying forth this deeply ingrained family tradition.

—*Sheila Hsia, Hong Kong*

# A Useful Dees-tour

*R*ecently, my sister, cousin, mother, and I traveled to Atlanta, Texas, in search of our roots. We spent the morning in the Atlanta Public Library's genealogy section, dividing the labor in an attempt to look through everything we could think of—obituaries, city directories, all the local history books, family files, and cemetery listings. Then we went to find the old cemetery to take pictures of any headstones of family members we knew.

It was a very hot, steamy day as we traipsed the rows sweating, snapping pictures, and looking forward to the air-conditioned ride on to the next town. Wilted, we all got back in the car and my sister said, "I just remembered that I didn't check one of the cemetery books at the library. There's probably nothing in it, but do you think we should go back to the library and check it?"

None of us lives within 700 miles of Atlanta, Texas, so we decided if we didn't check it then, we never would and then we'd always wonder. We returned to the library and plopped ourselves down in the genealogy section. My sister retrieved the missed cemetery book while the remaining three were happy to just sit.

As we sat, a member of the local genealogy society came up to us, said she was volunteering that afternoon, and asked if she could help us with anything. We said no, we were looking for the Dees line and had just come back to check one more book. She replied, "Oh? My family line is a Dees line."

We set upon her with questions and quickly discovered she was not *our* Dees line, but then she said, "There is another Dees line here in Atlanta. Have you called Mildred? Her maiden name was Dees and, although elderly, she's in excellent health."

We nearly knocked each other over getting to a phone to call Mildred. Yes, she was ours! Her grandfather and our great-grandmother were brother and sister. A link we thought was lost welcomed us into her home that evening to share information.

Was there any information in the missed cemetery book that drew us back to the library? No. But being thorough, reluctantly returning to the library, and checking that overlooked book connected us with a living branch of our family tree. All in all, we decided it was well worth the Dees-tour!

—*Sally Kading, New Mexico,*
*and Betty Robertson, Arizona*

# Tombstone Detective

*M*y story begins with a search for my great-great-great-great-grandparents, James Campbell Bradshaw and Charlotte Organ Bradshaw. We knew that they died in Wilson County, Tennessee—James in the 1880s and Charlotte in the 1870s—but had no definite dates.

This prompted us to track down living relatives who might still be in the area. After several weeks, I found a woman who turned out to be their great-granddaughter. Annie Laura proved to be a walking history book, so my wife and I decided to visit her.

We spent a few hours looking through old pictures and Bible records. The visit took an unexpected turn though, just as we were saying our good-byes. We were already in our truck when I asked Annie Laura if she knew where James and his wife were buried.

She said, "Yes, they're buried right across the street along with most of their children." I looked over my shoulder and saw an old family cemetery. I couldn't pass up this opportunity and asked if I could go take pictures. She said she wouldn't mind, but I wouldn't find James and Charlotte.

When I asked why, she exclaimed that someone had taken the tombstones about twenty years ago. I stopped my engine and got out to hear the rest of this story. Apparently, a much younger distant cousin had lived across the street with his mother. When his mother died, the property was sold. Annie Laura said she was almost certain that this young man had stolen the tombstones when he left.

She had heard that he had moved to Knoxville and tried to locate him. A few years ago, her son had even volunteered to take her to

Knoxville. They were able to narrow the area down to a particular subdivision, and spent hours blindly knocking on doors inquiring about this man's whereabouts. The search was in vain, so Annie Laura resolved to put the past behind her and forget the stones.

I quizzed her briefly about this man. She told me his name and that he was a hairdresser with his own shop. When I got home, I found him in the phone book. Then I pulled out a map and located his street. The phone book didn't list the exact number, just the street. I must have called twenty times, but no one ever answered. Finally, I decided that if these stones were ever going to make it back to Wilson County, I was going to have to go and get them.

One Saturday morning my wife and I made the trip to Knoxville. We found the street and spent half an hour riding up and down, trying to pinpoint the location. It was completely residential, so it was apparent that he must operate his business out of his house.

We were getting nowhere, so I decided to stop at a nearby minimarket. I went in, bought a couple of sodas, and asked the gentleman behind the counter if he knew of this man. I told him that my wife and I had just moved to the area, she was looking for a place to get her hair done, and a neighbor had suggested this fellow. He was more than happy to give us the exact address.

Armed with this information, we made our way down the street to his house. We drove by and saw no cars or activity, so I tried calling on my cell phone. He answered and I hung up. We waited about ten minutes and then went to his door and knocked. I knew someone was there, *Rescued tombstone of Charlotte Bradshaw.*

but no one answered. Finally, a neighbor came out and said he was probably in his shop at the back of the house.

I went around to the back and knocked on his basement door. At first the man who answered the door seemed a little nervous and wouldn't admit to being the person I had asked for. While exchanging small talk, I began looking around his shop. To my amazement, sitting on the floor with a vase sitting on top of it, was a part of James's stone!

I questioned him about it and he started to get angry. It was then that I informed him of my real business with him. I told him that I had contacted the police and was prepared to have my wife phone them if I did not come back out in five minutes. We walked out to the street where my wife was waiting with phone in hand. He recognized that his theft had finally come to an end.

I told him that he had three choices: He could take the stones back to Wilson County and explain why he had taken them to begin with, I could take them back to their rightful place, or I could call the police and let them decide what to do. He immediately thought that my taking them back was just the

"*Tis father's grave!-well may his memory live!*
*I charm to this loved spot his mum doth give.*
*Long will posterity his virtues own.*
*When blank or broken is this pillar'd stone.*"

right choice. As I loaded the stones in my truck I thought about just letting this guy have it, but chose to get in the truck and take them back "home."

Later that afternoon I pulled up to Annie Laura's house and asked her to come out to the truck. As I pulled back the tarp, she began to cry, so overcome with joy was she to have the stones back where they belonged. We took the stones to the cemetery and I placed them in the positions she indicated. The stones had finally come back after twenty years of being used as decorations in a Knoxville basement.

Annie Laura told me that God works in mysterious ways, which I believe he does. She said that I was sent to her to find those stones. I don't know if that's true or not. What I do know is that it was one of the warmest feelings I've experienced in my life, and I was more than happy to see my great-great-great-great-grandparents' memorials back where they belonged.

—*Jace Jackson, Missouri*

# Where Did All the Flemings Go?

*I* had been researching my own family history here in Australia for about ten years when my father-in-law, Charles Fleming, asked me to research the Fleming family. He mentioned that he had relatives living somewhere in America, and that the last contact with them had been about 1918. As proof, he produced a letter written in 1918 by Matilda Fleming-Barr, apparently an aunt of his, from Philadelphia, Pennsylvania. He also shared the useful tidbit that there was a Presbyterian minister in the American branch of the family—Samuel Fleming Sr. It was now more than half a century later. Could I possibly find traces of these people?

I began by going to the American Consul in Queensland, Australia, to copy the pages in the Philadelphia telephone directory that included the names Fleming and Barr. It was clear I was in for quite a challenge as there were 195 Flemings and 112 Barrs. I decided to chip away at this list by sending twelve letters to Philadelphia each month: six to Flemings and six to Barrs. I received many answers, but found no apparent connection. I also wrote twice to the Presbyterian Church in the United States, but they informed me that they had no record of Rev. Samuel Fleming Sr.

After 136 letters, I was about to give up my search. Where had all the American Flemings gone? Thankfully, it was just about this time when I received a letter from a Dorothy Fleming of Philadelphia saying she was not related but would like to try to assist me. Her neighbor's mother worked for the Presbyterian Christian Board, and she had asked her to check the records to see if there was a minister by the name of Samuel Fleming anywhere in America.

Dorothy's friend managed to locate a Rev. Samuel Fleming *Jr.* in a little church in Milford, New Jersey. Thinking I was looking for Sr. rather than Jr. had caused my earlier inquiries to the church to come back negative because I was unknowingly several decades off in my timing. Samuel Jr. was not ordained until 1941.

Dorothy called Samuel Jr.'s number and spoke to his wife, Annie. According to Dorothy's letter relating the conversation, she really quizzed Annie:

> *I called Reverend Fleming and spoke with his wife, and asked her was her husband from Philadelphia, specifically Germantown, and she said yes. I asked did he have a sister Matilda and she said that was his aunt. I said was she married to Robert Barr with a grocery store on Germantown Avenue. She said that is exactly right. I said someone in Australia would like to hear from you and I went on to tell them about your letter. I said I just did not want to let it go unanswered like the other 88 or 89 people. The least I could do would be to try and get you some information.*

Dorothy had succeeded in finding our elusive American cousins! A short while later I received a letter from an elated Rev. Samuel Fleming Jr. We continued to correspond regularly until he and Annie came to Australia to meet us at a Fleming reunion in 1983. It was clear we had the right Flemings because they had the same family photos as we did! Reassembling the family, we now understood why it had been so difficult to find our Flemings in America. From the one Fleming, William, who had emigrated to Australia, there were now three hundred descendants, but from the five Flemings—Joseph, Samuel, Matilda, James, and Thomas—who had gone to the United States, there were now only about ten living descendants. I'm glad I didn't know that when I started my letter writing campaign!

—*Kevin Slattery, Australia*

# Serendipity and Persistence

$\mathscr{D}$etermining the vessel on which Scandinavian immigrants crossed the Atlantic between 1860 and 1920 is usually a routine exercise in genealogical research. However, I learned to my sorrow that this is not always the case when I attempted to discover the name of the ship on which Lars Petter and Wilhelmina Karolina Storm, the grandparents of my wife, Marjorie, came to America.

Maine's 1900 census states that "L. P." and "Mina" had arrived in the United States in 1888. Based on this, I borrowed the microfilm containing the 1888 police records of Göteborg, the port from which the majority of Swedish emigrants embarked on the initial leg of their journey to North America. I ordered the police records, not because Marjorie and I suspected that her grandfather was a criminal, but because the law of the land decreed that before a ship with emigrants sailed from any Swedish port, its captain was required to submit a list of those emigrants to the city's police authorities. Inspection of these records revealed that on July 6, 1888, the Storms and their sons, Lars and Carl, along with sixty-six other Swedes and thirteen Finns, boarded the SS *Orlando* at Göteborg for the stomach-churning voyage across the North Sea to Hull, England. If they followed the usual travel pattern, they then rode four hours by rail across England from Hull to Liverpool where they embarked for New York.

This reasoning prompted me to order the microfilm of passenger lists of ships that landed in New York during the final two weeks of July 1888. Although I found the names of hundreds of Swedes aboard ships that had traveled from Liverpool during that fortnight, I found no Swede bearing the surname Storm on the microfilm.

Completely stymied and deeply disappointed, I concluded that I was pursuing a lost cause, but serendipity, in the form of a conversation with my brother-in-law, Louis Larsson of Presque Isle, Maine, came to my rescue.

Louis recalled that when he was a child, his grandmother Wilhelmina told him of a violent storm during which a sailor was killed when he crashed to the deck from the mast of the ship on which she and her family sailed to the United States.

Although I was pessimistic about locating information concerning the accidental death of a common seaman aboard ship thousands of miles from his home port more than a century ago, I e-mailed the Cunard Museum at the University of Liverpool asking if that institution's archives might contain a record of the tragedy that had occurred during the latter part of July 1888. To my amazement and delight, I received the following reply from a dedicated curator who must have spent hours digging through the museum's old files on my behalf: "Leigh Lyon, storekeeper, SS *Aurania* of the Cunard Line, died on July 23, 1888, when he fell down Hatch No. 5 as the ship entered New York Harbor in rough weather."

While the sailor's death did not occur exactly as Louis had remembered his grandmother's account, I reordered the microfilm of the passenger lists I had examined previously. Upon obtaining the film I searched the *Aurania*'s manifest line by line, this time discovering Lars and Wilhelmina Storm and their young sons listed in Steerage Compartment 3. My earlier failure to find their names was partly my own fault and partly that of the purser, who erred by listing the members of the Storm family as being Norwegians rather than Swedes. My own culpability lay in the fact that in attempting to save time during the earlier examination, I had carelessly ignored the names of any passengers who were not designated as Swedish.

Serendipity, help from a family member, and a dedicated archivist in another country bailed me out when I had violated the law of scrutinizing every bit of available evidence with utmost care when conducting research into family history.

—*Edward F. Holden, New Hampshire*

# Digging for Roots

*W*e knew it *had* been there. "Jacob Collins, d. 1795 at the age of 45 years." That's what the 1930s Works Projects Administration cemetery survey says. It also gives the location of the marker in the Collins Cemetery in Lincoln County, North Carolina, and tells that Jacob's wife, Mary, was also buried there.

Danny Collins, my distant cousin and fellow researcher, found the cemetery several years ago, deep in the woods near a creek. At that time, all he could find was Mary's tombstone, lying on the ground, and about twenty other graves marked only with field-stones. He arranged with the landowner to get Mary's tombstone reset, but was unable to find a trace of Jacob's. Had it been van-dalized or destroyed by the horses that roamed the area? Or had someone actually stolen it? The remoteness of the area made it seem unlikely that anyone would try to carry something so heavy so far. And if it had been destroyed, surely a few broken pieces would still be lying around. Danny determined to come back to look further.

Several years passed before that opportunity came. Finally, Danny, my husband, Logan, and I made plans to make the hun-dred-plus-mile trip to continue the search. Knowing we probably would be dealing with thick undergrowth, we packed an assort-ment of tools.

Actually getting to the cemetery was in itself an adventure. After we found the right road and owner's home, we had to lug our equipment through a muddy pasture, sidestepping the horse and cow patties, and down to a creek. The creek, swollen by recent rains, offered a choice of wading through its swift waters or balancing on an old, rickety footlog. We opted for the footlog,

*Danny Collins and Logan Merritt poking and digging for clues.*

though the several subsequent crossings during the day never allayed my fears entirely.

Across the creek was another pasture with horses, then a copse of thick woods, and then a river. Danny remembered that the cemetery stood atop a circular knoll deep in the woods, enmeshed in a snarl of trees, vines, and briars. If he had not known where to look, we probably never would have found it. We had to cut a trail through the brush, so the going was slow.

Finally, we located the knoll area and stumbled onto a couple of fieldstones. Using our tools, we hacked a little clearing and uncovered more fieldstones. After working most of the morning, we had disentangled fieldstones for about twenty graves. Almost in the middle stood a "store-bought" stone engraved with the name Mary Collins—my great-great-great-great-grandmother!

What a feeling, as I stood there and tried to imagine those who lay in the ground around me! Who were these who only had fieldstone markers? What had their lives been like? Who had gathered here, around each grave, to say their final good-byes? Knowing that this was a *family* cemetery, *my* family, brought a strange sense of belonging to the scene.

*Danny Collins with unearthed tombstone of his great-great-great-great-grandfather.*

Danny showed us where he had found Mary's stone, lying on the ground beside a tree, and said the landowner had reset it, not really knowing the exact location of her grave. Apparently, he had chosen a spot where the digging may have been easier than among the tree roots, since it now rests several yards from where Danny originally found it.

There was no sign of Jacob's stone, though we searched the entire area diligently. Danny was *convinced* it must be here somewhere. By now, it seemed that finding it had become an obsession with him. We decided to poke into the ground across the hill. We used screwdrivers, a bush hook, and a machete, sticking them into the dirt in a pattern, at intervals of about a foot, hoping to feel something hard. The sun grew hotter as we steadily worked, until we voted to take a break for lunch. Knowing we still had a return trip ahead of us and wanting to make every minute count, we did not rest long. With renewed fervor, we poked feverishly and with little conversation.

Suddenly Danny's hook made a sharp, scraping sound! With bare hands, he began pawing into the ground, throwing dirt behind him like a dog digging for a bone. Logan and I joined in, carefully moving dirt so as not to damage anything we might find, yet hurrying with expectancy. As Danny uncovered a broken corner of what obviously was part of a tombstone, he began literally to tremble with anticipation.

Gradually, we unearthed a flat stone slab and pried it from the clay that had encased it. With shaking hands, Danny eagerly scraped away the dirt. We used our remaining drinking water to wash out the depressions of the engraving.

As the first name began to appear, Danny's shriek could be heard across the hillsides! "We've found it!" He jumped up and down and grabbed me in a bear hug with pure abandon. The look on his face was one of unbridled joy. Exuberantly, yet almost reverently, he fingered the letters that spelled out our ancestor's name. The stone, which had been broken off about ground level, had been lying flat under about three inches of dirt, a piece of history probably lost forever had it not been for Danny's persistent quest. It seemed only fitting that Danny should have been the one to make the discovery that day.

We searched the area for the base of the stone, but never could find it. Danny speculated that since Jacob's tombstone was also close to the tree where he had originally found Mary's, their graves might have been disrupted by the growth of the now-huge tree. We located two depressed areas in the ground there that possibly could have been graves.

It was growing very late, but since we had a shovel with us, we decided to reset Jacob's stone in the depression nearest the tree. We would have to return later to move Mary's to the depression beside it.

With the stone once again erect, we picked a bouquet of wildflowers, placed it on the grave, and observed a moment of silence in respect for the one whose blood still flows in our veins. After recording the entire scene thoroughly with several photographs, we gathered our belongings for our journey home. Our feelings of excitement, triumph, and satisfaction far outweighed the pain of our tired muscles and aching backs!

—*Ann Collins Merritt,*
*South Carolina*

*Jacob Collins's repositioned tombstone.*

# Dusty Memories

*W*ould you believe me if I told you that one of my most prized possessions is a transparent red key chain from an auto repair shop? No, I'm not a collector who became bored with matchbook covers and candy dispensers. And no, it's not made of ruby or some semiprecious stone. In fact, it's rubber. Maybe I should start at the beginning.

When I was about five years old, I went on a trip with my grandparents to Wilkes-Barre, Pennsylvania, the city where they had been born and raised. On the way, we passed an auto shop with "Smolenyak's Auto Body" painted on one wall. I couldn't read very well yet, but I knew my own name when I saw it, so I excitedly asked my grandparents about it. For whatever reasons, they quickly dismissed it. Being an obedient child, I let the subject drop.

Over the years, the memory became increasingly faint to the point that I almost thought I had made it up. But a part of me persisted in believing it, and it was this part that kept me looking for other Smolenyaks and checking the phone book in every town I passed through on my extensive travels. I had begun my obsession with genealogy as a sixth-grader, just about five years after this episode, but after twenty-two years of searching, was just about ready to give up on ever finding any other Smolenyaks. I had tried all the other usual tactics—vital, church, census, newspaper, military, ethnic, and other records—but still had nothing to show for it. Still, that dusty childhood memory lingered in the back of my mind and wouldn't let me give up the hunt.

When the first large genealogical databases became available on CD, I paid to have lists with my surname printed out and sent to me. Still no clues. But finally, the Social Security Death Index became available on-line, and I could search it myself! I typed in "Smolenyak" and was almost delirious to find two "hits" for names I didn't recognize. I noted the zip codes and found them both to be in the Pen Argyl, Pennsylvania, area. Taking advantage of having an unusual name, I called Information in this area and got several listings for Smolenyaks and Smolenaks. On my second call, I reached Mike Smolenak, who had also been researching his family for years and had almost reached the same conclusion about being the only ones in America. I now had a distant cousin and genealogical playmate!

Finding each other opened the floodgates in our research efforts. Because we found so much information, we started the Osturna Family Association and a newsletter to share the findings. We shifted the focus of our research from just our own surname to that of our village of origin because we quickly realized that everyone in this little village of two hundred and fifty souls was ultimately related to each other! The readership now stands at about three hundred households—in the United States, Canada, Slovakia, and Czech Republic—and we recently started a Web site to make it still easier for Osturnites to share news and photos.

The most remarkable experience, though, was in 1996 when a gang of boisterous Americans took a reunion trip to Osturna in Slovakia. Thirty-seven Americans whose parents, grandparents, or great-grandparents had come from this village went back to meet

*Andy Smolenyak in front of his auto body shop in the 1960s.*

our cousins for the first time. We were genealogically blessed when we discovered that the mayor was a Smolenak who was delighted with the onslaught of American cousins—and even made Mike and me honorary citizens. We were entranced to find that the village had been historically preserved decades ago and consequently looked like "the land that time forgot"—just as it had been when our ancestors emigrated. And it didn't hurt that the village was nestled in the picturesque foothills of the Tatra Mountains and was wonderfully quaint.

So what does all this have to do with a key chain? On the reunion, one of my fellow travelers was none other than Andrew Smolenyak, the man who had owned the auto shop that had kept me looking for all those years. He told me that I had great timing since he had closed the shop shortly after I spotted it as a young-ster. Andy gifted me with a "Smolenyak's Auto Body" key chain, which I consider to be symbolically appropriate as it opened the door for me to hundreds of cousins! And that is why a red rubber key chain is one of my most treasured possessions.

—*Megan Smolenyak, Virginia*

*Mayor Jozef Smoleňák in center gives honorary citizenship to Megan Smolenyak and Mike Smolenak.*

# Diary of a Diary Quest

$\mathscr{I}$ was lucky. My great-grandfather left a tiny slip of paper to my grandmother upon which he'd written the townland from which our family originated in Ireland. It also included the name of his uncle, who just happened to be famous. That scrap of paper, given to me by my grandmother just before her death at age ninety-five in 1990, was the catalyst that took my Irish genealogical line back to 1685!

I began my journey of discovery by going to the Family History Library in Salt Lake City. When I showed the paper to the friendly attendants, they helped me find the famous uncle, "Honest John" Martin, in *The Dictionary of National Biography*. From this book, I found that he had been a member of Parliament and was known as "Honest John" because even his opponents knew that he would never speak anything but the truth. He fought for Irish Home Rule and was a Young Irelander. Researching the Young Irelanders, I learned that John was accused of treason and sentenced to exile in Tasmania.

On a return trip to Salt Lake City, I focused on researching the records of the church the family had attended, which had been built on land they donated. After three days, I had found very little and was frustrated. I

*"Honest John" Martin.*

repeatedly tried to find a particular book on this Donaghmore Presbyterian Church by a Reverend Cowan, but every time I went to the shelf, it was missing. Just as I was giving up to go home, I literally heard a voice telling me, "Stop! Turn! Look!" Right there in front of me was the book for which I had been searching! It had been misfiled by the title instead of by the author's name.

I quickly took it back to my table and looked in the index. Sure enough, there was the name of my famous ancestor! Quickly scanning it, I discovered that Reverend Cowan had a genealogy for both of Honest John's parents! I began crying uncontrollably.

Just then my husband returned to pick me up to go to the airport. I shoved the book in his hands and told him that we needed to copy every page before we left. He repeatedly stood in line, copied the permitted five pages, and cycled back to the end of the line to patiently wait his turn to copy another five pages. What a gem of a man he is! The book was four hundred pages long so we barely made our flight!

After reading Reverend Cowan's book, I discovered that he had gotten most of the genealogical information from the diary of one James Harshaw, an uncle of Honest John's. I wanted to read those diaries!

I went on-line and asked a simple question: "Has anyone heard of the Harshaw diaries?" A thoughtful stranger saw my query and forwarded it to Marjorie Harshaw Robie. Marjorie had recently been on a national morning show discussing the recently discovered Harshaw diaries—news to me!—and this woman had scribbled down her e-mail address. As it happened, Marjorie was in Ireland at the time donating the diaries back to Ireland, but her husband told me that Marjorie had arranged to have a microfilm copy made.

The story of the diaries is a miracle all by itself. James Harshaw had written them during the 1840–1867 time period. They contain detailed information on the weather, the church sermons, and every birth, death, and marriage of anyone he knew. After his death the diaries wound up with distant cousins in Pennsylvania and were deposited in the basement of a bank where a cousin was the manager. After the cousins died, the diaries were forgotten. Around

1985 the bank decided to clean out the basement. An employee was instructed to burn the diaries, but wisely decided to call the only Harshaw in the phone book. Sally Harshaw Lowing was at the Harshaw Realty Company when the call came through, and reluctantly agreed to take the diaries. They sat in her office, untouched, for a number of years.

In the meantime, Karen Harshaw Hickey of Iowa had begun doing research on her Harshaw line, as had Marjorie, who lived in Massachusetts. In the course of her research, Karen called the Harshaw Realty Company. Sally told her about the diaries and even lent her one. Karen eventually got all six volumes, but could make no connection to her own Harshaw family. She did, however, recognize their worth.

Just about then Marjorie put a feeler out by mailing letters to every Harshaw she could find in the eastern United States. Karen answered Marjorie and eventually shipped the diaries to her. Marjorie began the tedious work of transcribing the six volumes, all thirteen hundred single-spaced pages! She also shared the diaries with the New England Historic Genealogical Society in Boston. They agreed to microfilm them and notified the Public Record Office of Northern Ireland (PRONI), which declared the diaries "the most important historical document in all of Ireland." It was a diary of a simple tenant farmer, but included items of infinite worth to the Irish people. PRONI invited Marjorie to return the diaries to Northern Ireland and Marjorie obtained Sally's permission to do so.

When Marjorie returned from Ireland, she and I talked on the phone for three hours as she filled me in on the amazing information contained in the diaries about my family. She agreed to lend me her copy of the microfilm, and I spent the next three months going daily to my local Family History Center to read the microfilm.

I read about the sentencing and transportation of Honest John under a new law making it a "treason-felony" for even implying that the British government was not taking proper measures to prevent the starvation in Ireland during the famine. I cried. I read about the deaths of Honest John's brother, Robert, and his wife, Millicent, nine days apart leaving seven orphaned children. I learned that Honest

John, a bachelor who had just returned to Ireland with a pardon, undertook the task of raising these children. I cried again. The names on my pedigree chart came alive. I wept with joy, admiration, and appreciation for the diary of a simple tenant farmer.

Best of all, Marjorie invited my husband, Russ, son Kevin, and me to go with her to Ireland for the dedication of the new headstone for this simple tenant farmer. There we met numerous Irish relatives. Because of the publicity about this event, others came forward to help me in my research, and I got to walk in the homes of several of my ancestors. One was over two hundred years old and still occupied!

So the ancestral quest that began with a simple scrap of paper led me to church records that led me to diaries that featured my family and only survived against incredible odds. I now have over eleven hundred ancestors' names entered in my software, but they aren't just names. They are people who walked this earth and their genetic material flows in my veins. I hear them calling me. I know them by name. I love and appreciate them and everything they did while on this earth. It is now an obsession to learn all I can about them.

—*Suzanne Ballard, Washington*

～ *Comment:* Excerpts may be seen at http://www.burgoyne.com/pages/ballark/John/Diary.html

*The scrap of paper that launched Suzanne Ballard's search.*

# As Clear as Mud

*I*f your research experience is similar to mine, you've spent countless hours in microfilm rooms staring at imperfect, sometimes nearly unreadable images. Old court minute books put me to sleep every time and the census isn't much better. Options? Not many. These are the tools.

I decided I had earned a field trip and settled on the family's old homeplace including possible surviving buildings and other memorabilia. I flew to Columbus, Ohio, and headed for nearby Licking County.

Around 1804, five generations ahead of me, Willis Lake married Nancy Grigsby in Frederick County, Virginia, and headed west with his new bride and, reportedly, one horse. Things kept getting better apparently, because around 1822, they purchased 100 acres of land in Hopewell Township.

Hopewell Township is decidedly rolling, with large hills, not unlike the land on which Willis grew up in Virginia. I had a township landowners map from an 1875 atlas with names, roads, and tract numbers, and quickly determined that the 1875 road pattern was pretty much intact. On arrival I found a good modern map, as well as an organized and friendly local genealogical society.

To get an inexpensive airfare, I had committed to a six-day stay. The week passed quickly with a day in the State Archives and a day or two in adjacent counties. I also drove the Hopewell roads several times, but the present landowners are weekend farmers now, commuting to jobs elsewhere during the week. Mostly there was no one to talk with so I was right back where I started—

researching in books. I did find several genuine, but unrelated, log cabins on these jaunts, but after five days of this I was pretty low.

My last day, Saturday—how could I make the best use of it? About noon I headed for Hopewell again. I drove down a narrow road, previously missed, and found an owner at home who knew his tract number. It was the one I was looking for. This was it— the old homeplace! Finally, I had a taste of success.

I asked the current owner about old houses. Yes, there was one up over the steep hill behind us. He warned that it was surrounded by timber and hard to locate. For two hours in ankle-deep mud I walked the length of that 100 acres and back, but there was no house that I could see. Deer hunters were banging away on the surrounding hills, but they missed me and the four-deer herd that regarded me from a safe distance.

Returning to my car with ten pounds of mud clinging to each shoe, I drove to the next farm hoping to walk in at a different angle. This was my first and only hostile reception the entire week. Probably to get rid of me the owner drove me in a four-wheel drive to where I could vaguely see the outline of the house, but wouldn't allow me to get out of the vehicle. From my vantage point it appeared to be a farmhouse with relatively modern-cut lumber, conventionally built in the late 1800s.

By then it was dusk. The friendly present owner of the old homeplace had mentioned a Mr. Rogers who still lived in the neighborhood, from whose family he had purchased his property. Should I make one more try, or go back to the motel and try to get the mud off my shoes?

Twenty minutes later I knocked on Mr. Rogers's door and explained my mission. "Yes, my grandfather bought that place from the Lakes. Did you see the old log cabin?" The hair bristled on my neck and I felt the pressure of rising excitement. "What old log cabin?"

*The elusive log home before it was encased in modern siding materials.*
*Shown is the Rogers family who bought the property from the Lakes*
*around 1889.*

We got in his car and headed back. As we drove up the headlights picked out a perfectly normal, modern-looking farm outbuilding. Flashlight in hand, we entered a log cabin—covered with modern siding materials. No wonder I had missed it. There no longer was any clay between the logs, but there it was—a genuine, weathered, real log building. And all verified. Mr. Rogers's father was born in the log cabin. Mr. Rogers played in it as a child, after it was vacated as a home. There was no question that this was Willis Lake's old homeplace.

It was a wonderful, successful trip. What a change from reading old minute books! I heartily recommend it.

—*Joseph Lake, California*

# The Traveling Bible

*I*n 1986 I began researching my maiden name, Clotfelter, a Pennsylvania Dutch name originally spelled Glattfelder. I began corresponding with a distant relative, Janet Zemanek, and we decided to work together to write a family history for later publication. So from my home in Missouri and Janet's home in far-away Wyoming, we proceeded to coauthor an extensive family history containing the biographies of most of the descendants of our great-great-great-grandfather, Jacob Glattfelder (later Clotfelter), who was born in Pennsylvania in 1780 and died in Nebraska in 1867.

The life of Jacob Clotfelter is truly an American epic. He broke away from the rural Pennsylvania lifestyle of his father and immigrant grandfather, and followed the very edge of the American frontier. He did it more than once, settling first in Tennessee, then in Illinois, and finally, as an old man, in Nebraska. In each location, he left an extensive paper trail, which enabled us to reconstruct the course of his life.

Our 846-page book was published in 1994. When Janet and I started our research in 1986, we set three goals: (1) to locate a photograph of Jacob, (2) to locate a family Bible, and (3) to locate living descendants for each of Jacob's married children. We agreed to stop all research on January 1, 1989.

In our research, we wrote hundreds of letters, traveled to distant locations, and made numerous phone calls trying to locate living descendants. Our very last research trail before our deadline led Janet to contact a descendant of one of Jacob's granddaughters. We had long before given up on finding a photograph of Jacob, let alone a family Bible, having already contacted all the living descendants bearing the Clotfelter name.

*The well-traveled Bible and spectacles of Jacob Glattfelder.*

What we found was a genealogical gold mine! We made contact with Jack Crawford, this last descendant, who was the owner of an old chest of family memorabilia, which he kept in his Washington home. Jack hadn't paid much attention to the contents of the trunk stored in his basement since the Clotfelter name had little significance to him. We later learned the Bible had been given to Jacob's granddaughter who had married a Crawford. Since then it had been passed down three more times in the Crawford family. By the time it trickled down to Jack Crawford, the Clotfelter name had become a mystery. Janet drove immediately to Washington to meet Jack and have a look in the chest.

She told me that words cannot describe the emotional high she felt upon looking inside. Not only did she find the elusive photograph of Jacob Clotfelter (an ambrotype taken in 1864), but there was the well used family Bible as well as Jacob's eyeglasses, comb, money belt, money box, old newspapers, land records, and many other items.

It was the family Bible that was the most impressive find. Jack graciously allowed Janet to "borrow" the Bible, a New Testament printed in Old German Schrift, an archaic style of writing. Janet brought the Bible to me in Missouri so that I could see and hold it, and then on to York County, Pennsylvania, to show at the annual Glattfelder reunion there. While at the reunion, we learned that the Bible had been printed in Pennsylvania in 1795, making it a very rare and valuable book!

Although Janet and I did not own the Bible, we both began to get offers from museums and libraries that had heard of our discovery and wanted to add the volume to their rare book collections. Although the Bible had remained in Jacob's trunk for many generations, Jack generously decided to follow our recommendation that it be placed in archival storage to preserve it from further deterioration. It was finally placed in the Archives of the Evangelical and Reformed Church in Lancaster, Pennsylvania. This site was chosen since other Glattfelder family documents had been permanently stored there. How amazing! The Bible—which had left Pennsylvania with Jacob in the year 1800, traveled to Tennessee, to Illinois, to Nebraska, and then to Washington—had now traveled full circle back to Pennsylvania 191 years later!

Janet and I were thrilled to have made such a find. And we are delighted that the Bible was placed in the church's national archives where it will be protected from deterioration and available for viewing by future generations. No longer hidden in a dark trunk, Jacob's Bible is there for all to see!

—*Ruth Camenisch, Missouri, and Janet Zemanek, Wyoming*

*Jacob Glattfelder's Bible.*

# Looking for Love

$\mathcal{W}$e began looking for our roots almost twenty years ago. A cousin asked my father to verify some old papers that had once belonged to his sister. When he could not, he set out to see what could be proven through research.

We took my aunt's papers and began writing for vital records and asking cousins for Bible records and pictures. This effort rewarded us with assorted genealogical treasures, but we arrived at a very stout brick wall beyond my great-grandmother, whose maiden name was Hannah Robison. According to her abstracted death certificate, Hannah's mother was Sarah M. Cone. Census records over several decades showed that Hannah's mother's name was Susan, not Sarah. To be safe, we looked for both Susan and Sarah Cone, but extensive research only led to a series of dead ends. There were several Cone families near the Robisons, but none of them had a daughter named Susan or Sarah.

Frustrated, we continued to write to county clerks and researchers, hoping for new ideas. One of them referred us to a historian who knew a man who was in contact with a woman in Canada about the same Robison family. Talk about genealogical networking! We made contact with the Canadian woman and corresponded for some time, exchanging information and old photos. Eventually, we got around to a picture of a couple with the surname of Clows, and asked if she might know how they fit into the family picture.

She immediately became quite animated. They were her great-grandparents, Catherine Jane and George Clows! Her excitement seemed to open the door to her memory bank and all of a sudden, she remembered a Bible record that she had squirreled away. The record clearly showed that her Catherine Jane was a sister to our missing Susan (*not* Sarah, as it turned out)! The startling discovery, though, was that the sisters' maiden name was not Cone, but Love.

Now spurred on, we wrote for a photocopy of the *original* death certificate for our great-grandmother Hannah. Sure enough, on the original is "Love" written in fancy script. Someone mistook it for "Cone" and that is how it was transcribed for the printed record. Armed with this new information, we were finally able to uncover documented proof for several generations simply by looking for Love in all the right places!

—*Mary Sandison Fox, Oregon*

# Little White Lies

$\mathcal{F}$or twenty-five years, we ate our Sunday dinners at Nona's house. Nona was our Italian-born grandmother who immigrated to the United States with our grandfather and their oldest children around 1920. Every Sunday, the entire family would gather to eat the traditional foods and talk in Arbresche, the language of the Italo-Albanian people. Nona was our physical and emotional link to the old country, to this place that was so connected to us, yet also removed by thousands of miles and nearly one hundred years.

When Nona died, she left us with a tremendous feeling of emptiness, a desperate need to reconnect with "our people" and to understand more about the life that our grandparents left behind. We were struggling to find something tangible, anything that might help to preserve that link, to re-establish that fading connection.

We tried to research our roots in Piana, our hometown in Sicily, but never succeeded in obtaining any records. Our mother tried to help, too, but was repeatedly told that the records had burned. After about fifteen years, we gave up any hope of finding records in Piana.

The whole family was frustrated at not being able to get any genealogical information, so the two of us decided to try a different approach. We would take our mother and Aunt Rose, who had been born in Italy, back to Sicily and see Piana for ourselves. Aunt Rose was reluctant, but we finally talked her into it.

When we actually arrived, we were greeted by our many cousins and Aunt Rose acted as if she had never left! One of the first family members we met was our cousin Graciella, who knew the local archivist and was convinced that the fire story wasn't true. After years of rebuffs, we were not quick to accept Graciella's

*Nona Lamonaco as a child with her mother, Guiseppa.*

word, but hoping against hope, a cluster of us descended on the Municipio to see whether the records really existed or not.

Within a few minutes of our arrival, Aunt Rose found her own birth record in a ledger! The records had not burned, but were very much intact. What we hadn't known is that an excuse such as "the records were burned" is considered the polite way to turn down requests that one simply doesn't have the time or resources to fulfill.

It's true that we could have gotten upset over fifteen years of fibs, but it was those little white lies that gave us reason to go to Piana. Without them, we never would have had the magical experience of meeting our cousins and discovering the original records ourselves. No mailed photocopy could have given us the sense of connection and belonging that we gained by visiting Nona's hometown. Just maybe it was all part of Nona's plan!

—*Jeff and Craig Gallup, Utah*

# Children of Manchester

*T*wo things happened in the late 1940s in Manchester, England, that would impact on each other halfway around the world over fifty years later. A young woman named Maud gave birth to a child and named him Terence. Due to her circumstances at the time, she placed him for adoption. And Manchester University gave birth to something called a "computer" and nicknamed it "Baby." Half a century on, one of the descendants of "Baby" would become part of what we now call the Internet, and this would be used by the other Manchester baby to find his birth family.

I remember stories of my adoption from my earliest recollections as a child. Nothing of these events was kept from me. There was, however, one piece of information that was simply overlooked, and this snippet of information was unearthed because I could not find my birth certificate.

In 1970 I emigrated from England to Australia, followed a year later by my adopted mum and dad. Many family papers were still with my dad, my mum having passed away in 1986. Having looked everywhere at home, I decided that perhaps my dad had my missing birth certificate.

I rang my dad and asked if he knew of its whereabouts. "Of course I do," he said. "It's in one of those shoe boxes in the wardrobe." My heart sank . . . I have seen that wardrobe. But to my surprise, he found it within an hour. He gave me the certificate as well as some other papers—the 1948 court order for my adoption and a letter they received from a Mrs. Tribe at the adoption agency. The letter was handwritten and difficult to read, but contained a few words that would change my life. In my parents' excitement of receiving the letter, which informed them that there was a child available for them, they missed this detail.

Lancashire and Cheshire Child Adoption Council
5 Cases Street, Liverpool 1

4.12.47

Dear Mr. and Mrs. Cooper,

There is a baby boy whom I think you may like to see.

Terence was born on September 15th weighing 7lbs 12ozs at birth &
he has a very good medical certificate. He has also a very nice mother
but unfortunately this is her second child. She was going to be married
to this baby's father before she met the father of her first child. She
seems to have been very fond of him at the time but when she was pregnant she wrote to her fiancé & told him. He came at once to see her, she
thought he would make a home for her baby & herself. However, now that
this baby has been born, the marriage is off definitely.

Terence & his mother are in one of the best mother & baby houses
that I know and the Superintendent tells me that she is one of the nicest
girls she has had. She is intelligent, & baby should be nice. He will certainly be well trained!

If you would like to see him, will you let me know, return of post if
you can come here on Friday, December 12th at 3:15pm prepared to take
him home with you if you like him? Will you bring a case for his clothes.

Yours sincerely,

D. Tribe

The words "this is her second child" almost jumped off the
page. I had no idea that I had a sibling and my father was equally
astonished. With the support of my father, wife, and children I
started to search for this other child, but wasn't sure where to
begin. The only information I had was my natural mother's name,
the name of the adoption agency in Liverpool, my birth date, and
my place of birth.

My initial efforts led me to discover that the adoption agency
was no longer in existence. Wanting to find out what happened to

it, I decided that the Internet would be a logical starting point. I quickly found that the cities of Manchester and Liverpool both had Web sites, complete with sections for public notices, so I placed notices in both.

I got lucky. Margaret, a lady in England, replied that her husband was adopted through the same agency. She also provided a good deal of information regarding the procedures involved, not to speak of help and encouragement in the coming months.

I now knew that after the adoption agency had closed, the files had been turned over to Liverpool Social Services. Anticipating problems in dealing with bureaucracy, I was in for a pleasant surprise. I phoned the office and was put through to a very efficient lady in the Family Placement section. I told Brenda what I knew. She said, "Just a minute," and was half of that when she replied, "Yes, we have your records. It will take about a week to physically get hold of them, because they're archived in the bowels of a building somewhere, but no problem."

She wasn't allowed to tell me any details, as it is necessary to be counseled prior to receiving the documents. It appears that in the past, some adoptees have not handled the information too well so this is the current system and we must abide by it. Brenda informed me of the agencies here in Australia to which they were permitted to forward the documents.

After due counseling and being cleared of suicidal or aggressive tendencies, I received my adoption notes. These included the application form that my birth mother, Maud, had completed, an unsigned letter outlining her situation, and a copy of my medical certificate at birth. At this time I also applied to Britain for my original birth certificate. In addition to what I previously knew, I now had the following information:

~ The name of the maternity home, St. Monica's
~ Maud's address in Manchester
~ Her place of work and occupation, Metal Box Co.
~ Her religion—Church of England
~ My sibling—an 18½ month old boy (in December 1947)

∼ My natural father's name and address; his religion—
   Roman Catholic; his age—twenty-one; and occupation—
   Royal Navy
∼ Maud's response to the question why it was desired to
   have the child adopted—"My income is insufficient to
   keep two children and I would not be able to bring them
   up as I would wish"

There was one flaw in my newfound knowledge, but that was
not to be discovered for some weeks. Armed with these new
details, I went back to the Internet and placed another notice in
the Manchester site. This time I was looking for anyone who knew
of Maud from the address that I had, who had worked at the
Metal Box Co. during and just after the war.

About this time I was running out of ideas, so I contacted a
local Family History Center to see if they could help. I spoke to the
center's director, Ray Thorburn, who reassured me that they have
helped many adoptees and that he was an adoptee himself. I made
an appointment to see him and Helen Wells. The help and encouragement I received from these two was invaluable. Helen, it turned
out, was also adopted and a fierce campaigner in Australia for the
rights of adoptees.

From the huge amount of information available at the center,
we discovered records of my birth, Maud's birth, and the birth of
my sibling who we discovered was a boy named David. We also
found that Maud was born in 1924 and had three sisters: Muriel
born 1917, Edna born 1920, and Irene born 1922. It later turned
out that she had another sister, Alice, but I missed her.

Important questions were now emerging: What will I do if and
when I find my mother? How will I break the news? How will it be
received? Will she want to see me? She will be getting on a bit
now. Will it upset her too much? All of these things had to be considered. Fortunately, Ray and Helen had been through this personally and on numerous occasions with other adoptees and were
immensely helpful in coaching me through the whole process.

My original birth certificate had arrived by now from England. I wasn't expecting too much from it as I thought that I already had the information it would contain from the other documents. However, on close inspection of Maud's address, it was clearly "Moorfield" Avenue, not "Mossfield" as it appeared from the original handwriting on the maternity home letter.

I found through a British phone CD that I could reverse-search phone numbers by address, so I looked up Moorfield Avenue and got the phone number for 100, Maud's old house, plus a few up and down the street either side. The CD was a bit out-of-date, and some of the numbers were disconnected, including the one at 100. I was hoping either to find a descendant still there, or to find the people who moved in when they moved out, thereby finding out what became of them.

I did find a lady at No. 96 who was an old friend of Maud's mum. She was now ninety-two years old and told me that the family had moved away years ago. Maud's mother had died and the girls had married and dispersed. She couldn't remember any married names, but thought that Muriel emigrated to Australia and had a little boy. She also remembered Maud. I had at last found someone who knew her. I was to later learn that my new friend was confused about which sister emigrated and to where, but blissfully unaware for the moment, I was delighted with this progress!

One of the searches that Helen suggested was to look up marriages of anyone with my natural mother's name between 1947 and 1964, by which time she would have been forty years old. We found two in 1948 and one in 1951. The first I tracked down to Lancashire, but it turned out to be a different lady of the same name. I could find no trace of the other two still in Britain today, so I returned once again to the Manchester Web site and posted another flurry of queries looking for the two or for anyone who knew my brother, David. I also revamped the older postings with the new, correct address.

Unfortunately nothing was producing results. It was as if the whole family had fallen off the planet. I had notices everywhere we could think of. Then disaster struck. Helen had a stroke on New Year's Eve. She lived for a few weeks, but was unable to survive a second stroke. I had lost one of my biggest supporters, and was beginning to lose hope as well.

But several months later, without warning, the world turned upside down. An Internet user from North Carolina by the name of Francis saw my postings on the Manchester site. He was raised in Manchester and looks there periodically to try to find old school friends.

I woke one morning and checked for any new e-mails, as is my habit when I have finished scratching myself. Four messages were waiting for me from Francis, all sent within a half an hour period, each responding to postings that I had made in the Manchester site. Collectively, they told a story of his mother . . .

～ Her name was Maud, and of the same maiden name.
～ Her married name matched one of the marriage records I found, but had no success in tracing in Britain.
～ She had moved to North Carolina in 1968 with her husband and children.
～ She had worked at Metal Box Co. during the war.
～ She had a son, David, who was born before she had met her current husband.
～ She had four sisters, Muriel, Irene, Edna, and Alice . . . and, apart from David and himself, there were other children—Ann, Marie, and Mark.
～ She had died in 1993, and is survived by her husband Frank who is seventy-eight years old and living in North Carolina.

What a way to start the day! I now had—without any doubt in my mind—three half brothers and two half sisters. Until a few months ago, I was an only child.

Now the dilemma. I knew for a fact that I had found my other family, but they didn't have this knowledge. What to do? There were several possible scenarios:

1. It may be common knowledge that their mum had another baby that she adopted out. After all, they know about David being born before she was married to their dad.
2. Perhaps Maud told her husband, Frank, about it, but never told the children.
3. She may have kept the whole thing secret. It would not be pleasant for Frank to find out that his wife had kept a secret like that all their married life.

Apart from that, what sort of reception was I going to get when I dropped this particular bombshell? It's an awful lot of people to have angry with you.

Then I remembered something that Helen told me: "When you find your family, remember that they are part of you. If you would welcome the news, they won't be much different and will probably welcome it too."

But that was for later. I had to figure out where to go from here. I decided to go see Ray and get his advice. I really thought that I would be calm and in control if this situation ever came about. Not a hope. I was a mess. After several cups of coffee, we decided that since Francis had been so open and helpful, the least I should do is be as honest with him, and worry about the consequences later.

As a prelude, I sent a return message. I was nibbling around the edges, trying to find out which of the possible scenarios applied, so I sent this message:

Hi Francis,

Thanks for the reply, and for all of the information that you provided for me. It is certainly a lot of coincidence. I would say that this is the family line that I have been looking for.

Would you know if your mother had any other children after David, but before she married your father? Thanks again for the help.

Regards,

John

I went to bed that night, but slept very little. Every possible out-
come was running through my mind. Up bright and early the next
day, I eagerly check my e-mail to find the following message:

Hello John,
I don't know about any other children, but you know how it must
have been back then. Dad or David may know something but have not
shared it. I have to ask . . . what are the circumstances behind your
search? Your question raises many questions. I look forward to hearing
from you.
Regards,
Francis

Nothing for it now. I would have to tell all, at least to Francis. I
did at least give him a way out if it was going to be too traumatic. I
responded as diplomatically as I could:

*Hello Francis,*

*I apologize for being a bit secretive, but it was for the best of
motives. I wanted to find out first if it was common knowledge in
your family about another child to your mother. It would appear not,
so I will confide this to you, and trust to your judgment whether you
want to make it known to your father and others. I will abide with
your decision. The reason I was reluctant initially is that if your
father is not aware of these facts, it may be distressing for him and
it may be wiser to say nothing of it.*

*These are the facts as I know them:*

*On 15th September 1947, a person of the same maiden name as
your mother gave birth to a son, Terence, at St. Monica's Maternity
Home, Kendal, Westmoreland, England. The birth certificate under
"Name, surname and maiden name of mother" has Maud's details
including her occupation at Metal Box Co. Under the column
"Signature, description and residence if informant," it states your
mother's name and address in Manchester.*

*Maud at that time was in a difficult situation, and applied to
the Lancashire and Cheshire Child Adoption Council to have the*

child placed for adoption. One of the questions on the application form asked, "State why it is desired to have the child adopted." Her reply, in her own hand was, "My income is insufficient to keep two children and I would not be able to bring them up as I would wish." This was late 1947. I think David would have been about 18 months old at the time. This must have been an incredibly difficult decision to have to make.

The Lancashire and Cheshire Child Adoption Council, on the 4th December 1947, contacted some prospective adoptive parents, who took to him at once, and on 15th April 1948, they were granted an Adoption Order by Strangeways Court, Manchester. Out of respect for his natural mother, they retained his name Terence.

I was that child . . . John Terence Cooper.

My adopted mother passed away in 1986, and my adoptive father is still alive, well, and playing lawn bowls at 86 years of age. This is a shock for me too, but a very pleasant one (the discovery that is—not the lawn bowls). I have always known that I was adopted, but only found out last August that I had a half brother, David. Now I am delighted to find that I have a total of three half brothers and two half sisters, not bad for an only child.

It is not my intention to open a Pandora's Box, particularly if it will cause any grief or tension in your family. If you think it is best to leave well alone, then this can remain between you and me. I am happy to have found what became of Maud.

The only things I would like, if possible, are some photographs of Maud and family at various times through her life, and any medical history of Maud, her sisters, and parents. I can never answer the common medical questions of hereditary disorders, and I don't know of any possible medical problems that could crop up, not only for me, but for my children. Which reminds me, if your father is aware of this adoption, you can tell him he has an extra three grandchildren. I look forward to your response.

Regards,
John

Done! I sat back and waited for the bang, or whatever. Then this arrived:

Dear John,

First, let me say how wonderful it is that we've made contact.

This morning I spoke with my sister Ann. She had heard years ago through the family grapevine that Mom had another child, but she knew little about the details.

Knowing how much Mom loved children, it must have been devastating to her to give you up. Ann told me that Mom knitted baby clothes for you. She did that all her life—after we were grown, she'd knit for neighbors' children.

Your extended family include David, Marie, Francis, Ann, and Mark. We had a baby brother Johnny who was born in 1957 with a congenital heart defect. He died about six months of age.

Mom died of a cerebral hemorrhage—it was very sudden. Otherwise she was in good health—a bit overweight most of her later life. David talked to Dad tonight. Dad said that Mom told him before they married about your birth and adoption.

Anyway John, we're all now aware of our new brother (we've never used the term "half"—no point in starting now!)

If you approve, I will pass your e-mail to Susan (David's wife) who is on the Internet. I'm sure they'd love to correspond too. Susan can fill you in on all your new nieces, nephews and grand nephew (her grandchild)! Just tell me if all this gets too overwhelming, and I'll tell everyone to back off a bit.

I promise to get you copies of photos and medical history stuff. There's so much to share with you, but I want to hurry and get this out to you now.

Sorry if this mail is rather disjointed. I'm overwhelmed. Be assured that this is a very welcome Pandora's Box. It will stir us all up, that's true; we'll shed some tears of sadness for the past, and share some tears of joy for the present. I'll write again tomorrow.

Yours,
Francis

This is the exact same feeling you get when your first child is born. You go from being a recently married man to a father in a few tension-filled hours. You have a huge grin on your face that takes weeks to fade. You find yourself telling total strangers about it, as if you are the only person ever to have become a father. You have forgotten where you parked the car. You look at the sky and know for a fact that the world has changed forever—at least your bit of it. It is *that* feeling.

This has been a success story. Not all adoption searches are. I was lucky. I had excellent help from caring, experienced people and received a warm welcome. And finding the present whereabouts would probably not have been successful without the use of the Internet. I doubt that I would ever have considered extending my search to the United States without it.

That is how one child of Manchester helped another. One day I shall meet my extended family . . . but that will be another story.

*—John Terence Cooper, Australia*

# PART FOUR

# The Kindness of Strangers

*N*o, this isn't the generic "Can you spare a quarter?" or "OK, you can merge into my lane" brand of kindness. We're talking serious kindness where folks have gone to extreme lengths to help people they will probably never meet.

Genealogists are some of the most generous people on this planet. Most members of this extended community have helped countless strangers over the years "just because." Some rescue family photos and Bibles from antique stores or flea markets and reunite them with descendants of the original owners. Volunteers at historical societies will take a personal interest in a query from a stranger and take the extra step of publishing it in a local newspaper or seeking out living relatives for the writer. Some Americans have benefited from the generosity of unrelated Europeans who have helped them in their research simply to show their continuing gratitude for the role of the United States in World War II.

Let's all hope that these specimens of random and not-so-random acts of genealogical kindness blossom into a full-blown epidemic!

# Memorial Day Is Every Day

*O*n Memorial Day, many of us spend time honoring those who have died. However, genealogists spend years researching, recording, preserving stories and pictures, and memorializing their ancestors.

I have been researching my ancestors for almost thirty years. In 1990, while attending the funeral of my wife's uncle, I met her ninety-nine-year-old great-uncle, Peter Fabricius. Visiting with him, I became curious about the ancestors of my wife, Janet Lang. Two of her ancestors—Jean-Pierre Fabricius and Elisabeth Weber—were emigrants from Luxembourg; however, I did not know their towns of origin.

In 1995 I placed an inquiry in a Luxembourg genealogy magazine asking for information about these ancestors. Soon after it appeared, I received a letter from Jean-Pierre Jung, who lives in Colmar-Berg, Luxembourg. He wrote in English, and enclosed copies of records documenting the birthplaces and dates of my wife's two emigrant ancestors. He even included English translations. Over the next several days I received two more letters containing photocopied records and translations. I immediately wrote Mr. Jung thanking him for his research. I enclosed thirty dollars to cover his expenses, although he had not asked for money.

In Mr. Jung's next letter, he first thanked me for the "greenbacks," and then commented on my sending him money:

> *Thank you very much, but please, please do not repeat it in the future. I am not doing research for any material compensation. Take it as my small personal tribute to the sacrifice of those GIs who fought during the Battle of the Bulge for the freedom of Luxembourg's people, and*

> *of those many thousands buried in Luxembourg ground*
> *at Hamm near Luxembourg-city, with their General*
> *Patton of the 3rd Army. My joy is in giving service to a*
> *U.S. citizen.*

I was very moved that Mr. Jung would feel such gratitude fifty years after the end of World War II; and that he still would be trying to repay the American people for their sacrifices in liberating his country; and that I, who was only seven years old in 1945, was receiving this gratitude. Mr. Jung has helped me appreciate much more the sacrifices made by those who worked and fought to liberate Europe. But there is more to my Memorial Day story.

In the early 1960s I worked as an intern at the Veterans Administration Medical Center, Des Moines, Iowa. The Chief of Prosthetics was Cyril Mayrose. I knew that Mayrose was the first GI wounded in the liberation of Luxembourg. On September 9, 1944, Sergeant Mayrose was reconnoitering in front of the Fifth Armored Division in Gen. George Patton's Third Army. He crossed the Belgium–Luxembourg border in an armored car and slowly approached the first Luxembourg town, the town of Pétange. As he came around a turn in the road, a German gun emplacement fired on his car, hitting it and starting it on fire. Sergeant Mayrose was able to crawl free, but lost his leg below the knee. After the war, Sergeant Mayrose was knighted by the Grand Duke of Luxembourg, and a plaque was erected at the spot where he was wounded. I thought Mr. Jung would appreciate this story, so I sent him a copy of a *Des Moines Register* article about Mayrose.

In his next letter, Mr. Jung began: "Dear Daniel, I remember the burned out armored car at the entrance to Pétange. During the Battle of the Bulge, I passed the wreck each day. I am born and raised at Rodange and fetched a jar of milk daily at the mill of Pétange." He continued in his letter to say that he saw his first GI "at a road intersection near Boulaide on Sunday Sept. 10th at high noon." That was the day after the attack on Sergeant Mayrose's armored car.

During the past year, Mr. Jung has sent more than one dozen letters and packages containing scores of documents and translations, including color photos he took of the former homes of my wife's ancestors.

These examples of Mr. Jung's gratitude, and his memory of Sergeant Mayrose's burned-out armored car, inspired me to write a letter to Mayrose. Sadly, his wife responded that he had died several years ago. However, she wrote that it meant a lot to her to know that the sacrifices of her husband and other GIs were still remembered and appreciated by the people of Luxembourg.

Long live the memory of Sir Cyril Mayrose, and the memories of all those who have sacrificed and died for liberty. And long live Jean-Pierre Jung, whose thoughtfulness and generosity keeps alive these memories.

—*Dr. Daniel Kortenkamp, Wisconsin*

# Reclaimed Freight

$\mathscr{I}$ recently received a box of pictures that had belonged to an uncle who died in Tennessee in 1977. Uncle Luke was an avid collector of photographs, and had pictures of many relatives, friends, and neighbors. I began the task of organizing the collection by sorting through the pictures and separating them into piles.

I found myself intrigued by several apparently older pictures glued to black pages from an old photo album. Whoever had glued them on the pages had labeled one, but only as "Moma & Daddy." A few other loose photos of two young girls were labeled in the same handwriting and identified as "Betty—age 2 and Me—age 3 yrs. 4 m." I didn't recognize these people and they didn't resemble anyone in our family. On closer inspection, these photographs stood out from all the others. Whoever these people were, their dress and surroundings indicated that they were fairly wealthy. Even if my uncle had ever had the occasion to meet people of such wealth, they would not have given him such pictures.

I was racking my brain trying to figure out who these people could be when I suddenly thought, "I'm probably torturing myself for nothing. These probably came out of that old junk Luke used to bring home from the depot." My uncle had worked at the train depot and was occasionally allowed to bring home unclaimed freight. It was the only place I could think of where he might have gotten the photographs.

Even more curious now, I tried to pry some of the pictures off the black pages to see if any of them had names on the back. How fortunate it was that a picture of the two little girls had their full names and ages.

I logged on to the Internet to do some detective work. Luck was with me as I found the family tree of Sarah Frierson Armstrong, which included several names matching those on the photos. The tree provided some names from the current generation, but in the interest of privacy, no contact information. So it took a little more sleuthing to locate the youngest daughter of one of the little girls in the photos.

It must have been the strangest call she's ever received. It's certainly the strangest I've ever made. I asked her if she was the person whose name I had found on-line in a family tree—yes. I asked if her mother's name was the name I had found on the picture—yes. I told her that I had some photographs I thought belonged to her and explained my tale.

She grew noticeably excited. She told me that her parents were deceased and that the family had left Tennessee around 1948. On that trip, they had lost a trunk full of the family's heirlooms that her mother, Sarah, had continued to talk about for years. Sarah was so sad about not having a photo of her own mother that when she found a picture in the newspaper that resembled her mother, she cut out and saved this image of a stranger, just to help ease the loss. Her daughter had never seen a picture of either of her grandparents.

What a pleasure it was for me to tell her that she would soon see them for I was looking at them as we spoke. I happily packed up the "lost luggage" that had been missing from her family for over fifty years and sent it "home"!

—*Hester Janisch, Texas*

# What's in a Name?

Some people complain about having unusual names, and some even go so far as to change them, but you'll never hear me complain. Let me explain.

Many years ago my father set out to explore our family tree. He hired a professional who reported that there was only one other Podmajersky family in the United States and they were not related. Dad never took it any further than that. About two years ago, I did a vanity search on the Internet and discovered that there were actually many more Podmajerskys in the United States than the professional had uncovered. I wrote to all of them by regular mail, but received no leads.

At this point, I wasn't even sure which nationality I was— Czech or Slovak. In my on-line surfing, I came across a Slovak-oriented site. I figured my chances were 50–50, so I decided to join. After a few hours of reading others' messages, I worked up the courage to post a query. In less than two hours, I received a few replies. One of them was from a woman who said she was somehow related, but was unsure exactly how. She went on to say that she thought my family was from the area near Myjava, PodBranc, and Sobotiste, as she had traveled there and seen many Podmajersky graves.

Based on this newly unearthed clue, I started performing on-line searches of Myjava and Podmajersky, and came across a fellow named Podmajersky working in Myjava. This seemed promising. I shot off a message, but it was returned by the system administrator saying that Mr. Podmajersky no longer worked there. I wrote back asking for help contacting Mr. Podmajersky, which he kindly consented to do. A short time later, the mystery Podmajersky wrote me a letter! I followed up with every fact I had about my family history, and prayed that he would find something familiar in the papers. I really expected nothing.

Several weeks later, I received a most surprising e-mail from Rev. Lubomir Batka of Sobotiste. It basically said, "Hi, I'm the minister at the church your family has attended for three hundred years. Some of your dates are a little off, but I can give you two hundred years of your family tree from my church books. Also, you have living relatives in the area." Poof! Instant genealogy!

But there was still more to come. Later that very same day, a fellow named Peter Podmajersky wrote a message to my wife inquiring about her surname. I wrote back with my newly discovered information. We compared notes and discovered we shared the same great great-grandfather! His great-grandfather had been eight years old when his brother—my great-grandfather—had set sail! I silently thanked Dad for not Americanizing our name.

So I went from not even knowing I was Slovak to discovering cousins on both sides of the Atlantic on the same day! And two centuries of my family history had been handed to me, an anonymous foreigner, by a generous churchman in the old country. God bless the Internet and those who indulge roots-hungry Americans!

—*David Podmajersky, New Jersey*

# An Honest Broker

*T*hanks to Ed Elliott's wonderful resource, pastconnect.com, the George Kerns Bible has been reunited with descendants of its original owners. I came across this 1828 German Bible at a flea market and purchased it along with a number of other books. Being a minister, I know well that family Bibles are priceless to the families whose roots are recorded in them. I wanted to get the Kerns Bible back into the right hands, but how?

As luck would have it, I came across Ed's site, an on-line lost and found for family memorabilia. I posted the Kerns Bible, providing a few details from the family records, and hoped for the best.

It wasn't long before I received a query. A woman named Jenni had spotted my posting and happened to know of a "newbie" to Internet research who was pursuing the family members listed in my message. Jenni made the on-line introductions, and Tanya Kief and I began exchanging e-mail. Although Tanya had just gone on-line six weeks earlier, she had been digging for her roots for three years and also had the benefit of her great-aunt Margaret's previous twenty years of research. It didn't take her long to provide proof that she was indeed a great-great-great-granddaughter of George Kerns, the Bible's original owner. She had heard there was a family Bible, but had no idea what had happened to it.

Convinced of her bona fides, I sent the Bible to Tanya's family. I was delighted that it had returned home, and felt even more content when I learned that Tanya's Great-Aunt Margaret was one of the recipients. Tanya, of course, was overjoyed and is now planning a family reunion as a result of her growing interest in preserving and sharing the family's heritage. She tells me that it left her speechless to hold something her ancestors had held almost two hundred years ago. Her husband and the rest of her family were duly impressed with the results she produced after a mere six weeks on the Internet! It's so clear that the Bible was meant to make its way to her hands.

I feel blessed to have been a part of this transaction, but it was Ed who made it all possible. He's a broker—a family memory broker—and I can't think of a better kind.

—*Rev. L. Edward Durbin, New York*

# Let Me Explain

*S*ometimes I'm bewildered by the people I know. If someone told me that their hobby was transcribing nineteenth-century bank application forms for posterity, I would be fascinated! My daughter tells her friends not to ask what I'm doing when they come over. She's afraid they'll die of boredom before I finish my first sentence. My husband just says I'm weird. My friends think it's a phase I'm sure to get over. Nobody gets it. Let me explain.

These aren't just boring little entries that have no meaning to anyone. They are a gold mine of answers for those who want to know something about those who went before us. The Emigrant Savings Bank Records have taken over my life. For several hours every day, I transcribe bits and pieces of lives that ended long ago so that people today can find out who they are.

My tools are simple. I use my scanner to enlarge images that are too small to be read. I keep a magnifying glass, a laminated New York City street index, a list of towns in Ireland, and a bottle of aspirin at my desk. I try to enter between ten and twenty records a day. This is no easy task. The entries are handwritten. The information takers had beautiful handwriting, but the scrolls and curls that look so lovely can be murder to interpret! In some years, the depositor was allowed to sign the register. I am sure the Rosetta Stone was an easier read.

Sometimes I get swept up in the accounts themselves. Reading them is like listening to the whispers of the dead. A woman, beaten by her father, begs the account representative to allow her access to the account, even though her father has stolen her passbook. A young girl works as a seamstress, even though she is blind in her left eye. Another is too deaf to hear the questions. This guy has two thumbs on his right hand. A woman's husband died in crossing, and she has six children. A soldier going off to fight the Civil War wants assurance that his wife won't be able to touch his money while he's gone. Not all of it is pretty, but it sure is real.

After its first year, the database now has four thousand entries. Although this is only a drop in the bucket, it is a good beginning. There are so many more stories to tell, and so many more accounts to be read and entered. These are the stories of the common person. On-line databases never have any of my folks in them. We were too poor to book passage on the *Titanic*, and the only blue blood in my line is in the horses we stole. I found my folks in these records, and when I did, I cried. I knew then I had to get them out where they could be seen by others. When I read about your great-uncle on Pearl Street, I know that he probably knew my father's uncle Sam. If your great-grandmother lived on Mulberry Street, she might have known mine. It was a smaller world back then, and I want it to live forever.

—*Monica Bennett, New York*

# Cellar Treasure

*M*y good fortune started the day Mr. Smith's wife told him to clear out the cellar because there, in the pile of stuff accumulated over a lifetime, was the original grant to my family's coat of arms.

It started a couple of years ago with a letter from England. Mr. Smith wrote to tell me my address had been forwarded to him by John Hartley of Lancashire. Mr. Hartley had sent a copy of a letter I'd written to him in 1991, inquiring as to his possible kinship with my grandfather, William Hartley of Catteral Hall.

On my first journey to England in 1991, I had the good fortune to visit the home in which my grandfather was born. Catteral Hall was now part of Giggleswick School. The day I visited, my Yorkshire chums told the school's headmaster that I was visiting from Canada, tracing my family's roots. They explained that my grandfather had been born in this house in 1868 and asked if I could go in for a look-see. The headmaster was very gracious and invited me in. I saw the sturdy wooden banister my grandfather and his siblings had likely slid down as children. And there, in the study carved into the stone above the fireplace, was my family's coat of arms.

I asked if there were still any Hartleys on the board of governors at the school, a position my great-grandfather had held many years ago, and was rather surprised when the headmaster said there were. He jotted down the name of a John Hartley of Lancashire, and bid me good luck.

I corresponded a bit with Mr. Hartley and even though we weren't related—the Hartley surname being as "common as muck" in that part of the world—he offered me his best wishes and kept my letters on file.

Half a dozen years later, Mr. Smith's wife would tell him to clean out the cellar. It seems that he had liked to peruse the merchandise at the old flea market at Covent Garden in London. About twenty-five years ago, he had come upon some old parchment documents at a vendor's table. Being attracted by the colorful details, the brass boxes hanging from the document, and its all-round good shape, Mr. Smith purchased the Award of Arms, by Garter and Norroy Kings of Arms, dated 13 October 1841, to John Hartley of Catteral Hall, Giggleswick.

Doing much the same as I had, Mr. Smith contacted Giggleswick School and was told of a John Hartley still associated with the school. He contacted Mr. Hartley and that's when my address was forwarded to him.

Mr. Smith wrote to me that he was not a member of the family, but would quite happily pass the grant on to anyone who could prove that they were a direct descendant. If no one could do so, it was his intention to pass the document to Catteral Hall.

I had, over the years, been in contact with the College of Arms in London and provided them with all the necessary documentation proving that I was the great-great-granddaughter of John Hartley of Catteral Hall. I quickly sent a copy of this documentation to Mr. Smith.

Several weeks later, the courier arrived. The grant was beyond expectation. Sure, it was a bit tattered and crinkled, but the brass boxes still contained the original wax seals, and the colors were still vibrant under the years of dirt and grime.

I sent a letter and a small token of my appreciation off to Mr. Smith expressing my gratitude for this priceless gift. He wrote back, "I should have said earlier, it was totally unnecessary for you to have sent anything other than reimbursement for the postage . . . I intended the grant to be simply the return of a family treasure."

When I took the grant to the restorer he said the document had "memory." He meant that it had been rolled up for years, likely in a dampish place. I had tears in my eyes, for the memory the document had given to me was of the members of my family in England, a century and a half ago.

—*Katherine Anne Hartley, Canada*

# Recaptured History

$\mathcal{I}$n the 1870s, my ancestors—Sioux Indians—were forced out of their homes along the banks of the Cache la Poudre River in Colorado and onto the reservation in Pine Ridge, South Dakota. Pressure had been building from Washington to take the Black Hills from the Sioux so that gold-seekers would be safe, and after Custer's rout in 1876, my ancestors were swept up in the aftermath. But I didn't learn this until just recently. I had grown up with rumors that my family had come from Colorado, but they were never more than that—rumors.

When I attended a family reunion recently, I learned of a book about the Bingham Hill Cemetery near Laporte, Colorado. Supposedly, some of my kin were buried there. I contacted the author, Rose L. Brinks, and ordered a copy. When I found my great-great-grandmother's name—Jennie Adams McGaa Brown—I couldn't wait to go see her grave for myself. Half-Indian and first married to William McGaa, she had died in the midst of the removal. Her son, William Denver McGaa, was born in 1859 and had been heralded as the first predominantly white child to be born in the new city of Denver. We've often wondered if the removal initiative was a contributing factor in her death, and it saddens us to know that her mother, Mary, was compelled to trade her property for a wagon and two mules to travel to the designated reservation. In the cemetery, she left behind her daughter, Jennie, and her second husband, Alphonse LaRocque.

I traveled to Laporte and found a pioneer cemetery that had been closed for forty years, but recently and painstakingly restored to a semblance of its original condition. It contained more than 150 graves—a mix of Hispanics, early Anglo pioneers, a French-Canadian trader, several half-Indians—and tragically, the children of all of these people. More than 60 percent of those buried in the cemetery were under the age of fourteen. Had I come a decade earlier, I wouldn't have been so fortunate to find this remnant from the past.

Speaking with Rose, I learned that she and her husband had bought their property in 1977. She was aware that there was an old cemetery adjacent to their land, but with nine children to raise, didn't have time to explore it. In 1987, the former owner of her land, by then a ninety-year-old woman, told Rose that she had once seen someone bulldozing headstones into a bordering irrigation ditch. That got Rose's attention, and she, in turn, rallied public attention.

The cemetery was on unowned land, so Rose knew the only way to protect it was to get public support. She succeeded in doing this and finding a few invaluable volunteers as well. Together they cleaned up the cemetery, which wasn't even accessible at the time, and created a pathway on the Brinks family's land.

As she examined the few remaining tombstones, Rose felt a need to do still more, so she undertook a massive effort to research the people buried there and write a history of the cemetery. No burial records were ever kept, but Rose was determined to learn about the lives of those beneath the unmarked stones. Through untold hours of digging in archives and libraries, identifying and locating kin, and searching for tidbits and photos of the cemetery's inhabitants, she slowly recreated their lives. She then took all this hard-found information and wrote and published a book at her own expense.

Some might find this endeavor perplexing, but as Rose explains it, her book is "not a morbid necrology, but a celebration of ordinary lives." And she relates to her subjects. She speaks of agonizing about the drowned child who was pulled from the irrigation ditch, of knowing how the mother of fourteen children struggled, and of cringing about the three little Robertson siblings who died in such quick succession.

As the one thousand copies of her book found their way to history buffs and descendants of the people buried in Bingham Hill, the descendants wrote, called, and visited Rose and told her more about their ancestors. Rose incorporated these new details into another edition of the book, and recently had to publish a third version to include all the new information she had gathered.

As if that weren't remarkable enough for someone who had no kin in the cemetery she had adopted, Rose took it upon herself to raise money for a stone monument to list the names of all those known to be buried there, including the hundred or so whose families had been too poor to provide headstones in the first place or whose headstones had been bulldozed or otherwise removed. She later raised more money to replace the cracked 1877 tombstone of Alphonse LaRocque, the stepfather of my great-great-grandmother Jennie and one of the first French-Canadian settlers in the area.

She greets visitors, ranging from local fourth graders on field trips to grateful descendants who have contacted her from their corners of the world. At last count, over ten thousand people from all fifty states and more than twenty countries had signed the guest book at the cemetery.

I am just one of those grateful descendants and cannot thank Rose enough. Recapturing that piece of my history was like a fairy tale for me, and Rose was its author.

—*Wyman Babby, Montana*

∽ *Comment:* If you think you might have ancestors buried in the Bingham Hill Cemetery, write to Rose L. Brinks at P.O. Box 710, Laporte, Colorado 80535 to learn more or order a copy of her book.

# Perfect Timing

Several months ago my eight-year-old son was scheduled to have a biopsy after a series of hard knots had appeared in his lymph nodes. A few days before the surgery I was trying to distract myself from the worry and decided to check my e-mail messages. I had several from some of the genealogy mailing lists I'm on, including one from a Fran LaChance of Ontario, Canada, asking if anyone had heard of Malignant Hyperthermia running in their DuPuy families. Fran explained that a medical study had been done in Canada, and that the condition is actually called DuPuy Syndrome there because it's so prevalent in people of this surname.

*Branden DePue being prepped for surgery.*

I immediately wrote to Fran and obtained the additional information she had on hand. I then began researching the topic on the Internet and scouring my medical books from nursing school to see that else I could discover. I learned that Malignant Hyperthermia is a condition that causes patients under general anesthesia to suddenly spike a high fever for no apparent reason. There is only one drug known to help. Some hospitals don't stock it and most do not keep it in the operating room unless there is a family history. Many people have died from this sudden fever and there is no test to determine who is at risk.

*Hale and hearty, Branden DePue*
*after surgery.*

I wasn't sure of my own family's predisposition, as no one in my DePue line had had surgery for several generations, but there was evidence that the DuPuy Syndrome had struck a relative who was four generations removed from my son. This ancestor's death certificate contained a frightening phrase—"death from anesthesia."

Fearing this might be important, I sought out my son's anesthesiologist when I checked my son in for his surgery. I told him about this hint of a family history, and he told me that this little piece of information could have saved my son's life. He assured me that no matter how far back it might be, they always need to know about a suspected susceptibility in order to have the drug on hand.

I will be eternally grateful to Fran for sharing that crucial information at just the right time. My son's surgery went fine and he is A-OK today, thanks to genealogy and his ancestors who were thoughtful enough to leave traces of medical history. I have found yet another compelling reason to keep up my family research—as if I needed one!

—*Leslie La Brie–DePue, Arizona*

# Newsworthy

Some years ago, I determined to find out where my Martin ancestors came from. At the federal courthouse in Portland, Maine, I discovered my great-grandfather's naturalization records which listed his birthplace as Burnham-on-Crouch in Essex, England.

At this point, there were several approaches I could have tried to learn more, but I opted for a strategy of writing to the town clerk in Burnham. He was unable to help me, which, I suppose, should have been the end of my story. But this kindly clerk took it upon himself to give my letter to the local newspaper, which in turn, published a query for me.

Several months after writing to the town clerk, I received a package in the mail from England. In it were copies of three articles that the newspaper had published concerning my heritage! Apparently, two of my father's elderly cousins had contacted the paper regarding my query, and the editor had found this newsworthy enough to run several articles! The newly found cousins who sent this package even included a photograph of my great-grandparents, which was taken in Portland, Maine, around 1900. My great-grandmother had evidently sent the photo to her brother who still lived in Burnham. It was passed down to his granddaughter and, after a "holiday" of about eighty years, had found its way back to Maine.

I was able to visit England shortly thereafter and meet some of my surprise relatives. Without the initiative of the town clerk and the thoroughness of the local paper, which made it a mission to document my heritage, I would not have been able to find my ancestors, a valuable family memento, or my Essex cousins who have been part of my life since finding them twenty years ago.

—*Jeffrey E. Martin, M.D., Maine*

# Pass It On

*I*t was early spring when it occurred to me that I needed to think of a gift to take to my sister and her husband when we went to visit in early July. It wasn't long before I decided that the best gift I could give them was a better knowledge of their roots. This was particularly true for my brother-in-law, as his mother had died ten days after his birth and he had been raised by an aunt and uncle.

I knew the city in which he was born, so I went on-line to likely bulletin boards, Web sites, and chat rooms, and started asking questions, mentioning his mother's and father's surnames. In a very short time I began getting responses, and one kind soul offered to go to the local historical society to copy relevant records for me. As time when on, I began hearing from still others who were researching the mentioned surnames or knew of people who were. Within six weeks—totally due to the kindness of strangers—I had a two hundred–plus–page genealogy of his family! What a thrill! When I gave it to him, I was acutely aware that I was delivering the effort of dozens of nameless faces who had pitched in simply because they could. I wish every one of them could have seen my brother-in-law's surprise and pleasure.

One of those nameless faces to whom I had written a thank-you letter saying I wished I could return the favor wrote back with the following message: "Favors are not to be returned, but are to be passed on to others." You can be sure I will do my best to keep this chain of kindness going!

—*Nancy M. Goodwin, Delaware*

# Worth the Wait

$\mathcal{T}$racking down my immigrant ancestor on my father's side began in 1980, back in the days when most of us were computer-less. Conventional mail services were our principal avenue of communication and the waiting between sending and replies was often long and tedious.

Since I knew he had served in the military, I began by requesting a copy of the Civil War record of my ancestor. I was truly astounded when his file arrived because of its great length, which I subsequently discovered was due to his having changed his name after entering the United States. In the correspondence, he recounted that he had changed his German-sounding baptismal name, Claus, to Carl because his birth name was ridiculed in this country.

At the time of first contact, Claus-Carl was a man in his sixties applying for his service benefits. A later letter in his file declared his name change with an attached letter from the pastor of *Der Kirche Zu Kellinghusen* citing his baptismal record as proof of his name at birth. It was written in German, but a translation had been provided. The documentation gave his birth and baptism dates, as well as the names of his parents and baptismal sponsors—a bonanza of information!

With the necessary tools in hand, I wrote to the secretary of the Church of Kellinghusen requesting that they examine the church records and tell me what could be found about my ancestor's family. Naturally, I enclosed a check for time and expenses. It was more or less like putting a letter into a bottle and casting it adrift in the Atlantic Ocean, as I had no idea whether the church still existed, nor whether there was someone there in a secretarial capacity to process the request.

As the years passed following my letter to Germany, I gave up hope of ever hearing anything, and just wrote off the expense as a good try, since there had been no answer. But then, one day almost four years later, I heard a rather loud plop through the mail slot in my front door. Running downstairs to investigate, I found a letter that began as follows:

*Dear Mrs. Wrage Gunn,*

*I beg your pardon to have kept you waiting you for a long time but now I'm going to answer your letter from 20.10.1980 . . .*

The letter was dated *"30 Marz 1984"* and carried my line back to Hinrich Wrage, my great-great-great-great-grandfather born in 1753! Attached to the letter were segments of a chart showing all the descendants of this ancestor down through my immigrant born in 1836!

The dear lady who had done this work said that she had had my letter translated, but there was no one to help her search the church registers. Consequently, on her own time, she had taken the many entries of the Wrage family across town to a copy facility, one by one, and accumulated the family for me!

It was truly a breathtaking act of protracted kindness to deal in this family for four long years, make record-by-record photocopies of each relevant entry, categorize the family units, construct an easily comprehensible chart for me to follow, and then mail it off to the United States! That was fifteen years ago, and I remain astonished by her tenacity and generosity to this good day.

—*Kay Wrage Gunn, Texas*

# A Restorative Hobby

$\mathscr{I}$ restore heirlooms to the families who originally owned them. It's not the most conventional of hobbies, but I can't imagine a more gratifying one.

One of my first forays into this pastime began a couple of years ago when I purchased a framed 1873 wedding certificate with two tintype photos at an antique store in California. It occurred to me that with a little sleuthing, I could probably find some living descendants of this mystery couple. The groom's name looked like John Swartu and the bride's name was Elener E. Wilson. Both were from Michigan and they had married in Athens on May 22, 1873, at the First Baptist Church. This was enough to get me started.

I went to our local Family History Center and tried to find John Swartu, but came up empty. I couldn't help but notice that there were a lot of Swartz names and that's when it dawned on me that I had probably misinterpreted the handwritten script. Now that I had the right name, I looked up John Swartz in the 1870 census.

Success! I found eighteen-year-old John living at home with his parents and was pleasantly surprised to find Elener Wilson and her family living at the next farm over. She was sixteen—the proverbial "girl next door"! Tracing them forward through census records, I found them still living in Michigan in 1920. So how did the wedding certificate wind up in California?

Armed with their children's names gathered from the census records, I had another go at the Family History Center databases. Bingo! There was "my" Swartz family. The woman who had submitted the information lived in California, but was unlisted. Because her surname was slightly unusual, it wasn't too difficult to get past this hurdle. There were only four listings for her name in

*1873 wedding certificate of John Swartz and Elener E. Wilson.*

our state and the first one I tried turned out to be her son. I begged him to call his mother right away and have her call me. Half an hour later, the phone rang.

Donna was related to the wedding couple by marriage and was doing research for her children. She sent me a lengthy history of the family, which included an article about the couple selling their farm in Michigan and moving to Los Angeles around 1920, so that explained the California connection.

I was getting close, but wasn't quite done, as I wanted to give this certificate to a direct descendant of the couple in the certificate. Donna and a distant relative were writing a book on the Swartz family, so I got in touch with this other researcher, Elma. Equipped with more names from both Donna and Elma, I made another search for phone numbers on the Internet.

When I made my first call, a very soft voice answered. I almost fell over when she said she was the granddaughter of the wedding couple! Ella was now ninety-seven years old, but she clearly remembered the certificate hanging on her grandparents' wall.

Obviously, the certificate belonged in Ella's hands, so a short while after, my husband and I took a vacation by train and included a stop in Michigan to reunite the certificate with the Swartz family. Ella brought out all the old photographs showing the bride and groom with their children, and other members of the family treated me to a five-course Mother's Day meal from the same dishes that had been owned by the couple!

So my mission was accomplished! Now it's on to the next case. Someone's got to return these ancestral mementos to their families. Why not me?

—*Sharlene Van Rooy, California*

# Crossing State Lines

$\mathscr{I}$ had been e-mailing back and forth with a gentleman named Chester, as it seems there is some long-ago connection in our families. In the course of our correspondence, I wrote about a cemetery that was related to my family history. It was located in Ohio, and as I live in Florida and work sixty to seventy hours a week, it seemed unlikely I was ever going to get a chance to go see it.

In a totally unexpected act of charity, Chester, who lives in Virginia, took a trip to the Ohio cemetery, and took photos of about seventy headstones for me!

Among them was the tombstone of the founding father of our family, John Waggoner Sr., which was wonderful to see. As I was flipping through the other photos looking for names I recognized, though, I saw another one that stopped me in my tracks. There was the headstone for Clark P. Wagoner, my own grandfather.

My grandfather and I were very close. I loved him dearly. I went to his one-hundredth birthday party in Ohio in 1991, and was indescribably saddened when he passed away shortly after that. I always regretted that I was unable to go to the funeral or see his grave. And because of that, I have spent many nights wondering where his grave is and how I could get to visit him. I have wanted to see his final resting place and spend some time talking with him.

To see this photo of his gravestone brought tears to my eyes. I am both amazed and grateful that Chester took it upon himself to go all the way from Virginia to Ohio to take photos for an on-line acquaintance, and especially for the unexpected gift of seeing my grandfather's grave for the first time. Thank you, Chester.

—*Chris Wagoner, Florida*

# Bi-Coastal Bible

$\mathscr{I}$ live in St. Andrews, New Brunswick, and enjoy volunteering at our local Charlotte County Archives, as I'm interested in history and genealogy. About five years ago I stopped at a little antique store in nearby St. Stephen to poke through old treasures from our past. The store was situated in a former country schoolhouse, the Crocker Hill School. I was pleased to see that the owner of the shop, Marcie Garrymore, had kept the interior in its original style.

While there, I noticed an old Bible on the teacher's desk and asked if I could have a peek. She gave me permission and I carefully opened it to the family register section. I was delighted to find the pages filled in with names and dates, which Marcie allowed me to copy. She explained that she had purchased the school building in 1968, and all the furnishings, including the Bible, had come along with the building.

When I returned home with my precious sheet of Murray names, I began searching to find out who they were, but was surprised to find no trace of any of them. It became a mystery that I tried to solve repeatedly over the ensuing years, but I continued to run into brick walls.

About five years had passed when a letter came to the Charlotte County Archives from Carole Confar of California. She was researching her mother's family name—Murray. The letter gave the name of her great-grandfather, as well as his birth and marriage dates. This last, she said, occurred on September 10, 1885. When I saw the Murray name, I immediately dug out my notes from the old Bible. There was her great-grandfather's name, Alexander Murray, married September 10, 1885!

The Archives had given me a batch of letters to answer. That evening I began with Carole's and wrote a long response, explaining how I had come across the Bible and that I knew it was safe and

*Genealogy page of Murray Bible*

being cared for. I kept thinking how happy she was going to be to receive my letter even though I felt certain the owner would never part with the Bible.

About ten o'clock, it occurred to me that it would take four to six weeks for my answer to reach Carole due to the various steps in the response process. Realizing that it was one of those "cheap nights" to call the United States and that it would be only six o'clock in California, I reached for the phone.

She answered on the first ring. I introduced myself and told her to sit down because I had a story to tell. When I finished there was no sound on the other end of the line. Then she sputtered out a few words saying it must be their family Bible. I could hear her emotion through the phone.

The next day we had another chat. She said she was so excited that she couldn't sleep and had called all the Murrays up and down the coast of California. There was actually a legend that when the three Murray brothers left Scotland, their father had given them the family Bible to take with them, but the family had long ago lost track of it.

I kept reminding her not to get her heart set on obtaining it because I knew its present owner was very attached to it. I visited the owner and told her about the Murrays. She graciously allowed me to take pictures of the Bible to send to the family.

After a while, Carole decided to call the owner of the Bible. At first, Marcie wasn't keen on parting with it, but appreciating how precious it was to the Murrays, she agreed for me to pick it up. As soon as I had it in my hands I sent Carole a joyous e-mail!

Her family pitched in for a ticket and her aunt's children chipped in for airfare for their mother. I phoned the mayor of St. Stephen, Allan Gillmore, who now lives in the Murray house, and he invited the two Murray women to Sunday dinner at his home.

I was the lucky one who had the pleasure of handing the Bible to Carole and her aunt Pat. As you might expect, they were thrilled. They stayed a week and returned to California with many warm memories. Since then, Carole has had the Bible rebound by a Franciscan monk, Brother Wenceslas, and sent me a picture of him holding it.

Carole, Pat, and I are now firm friends, corresponding regularly, and I'm sure we have not seen the last of each other! All of us are grateful to Marcie, who agreed to part with a personal treasure to reunite it with the family who had lost it all those years ago.
—*Shirley O'Neill, Canada*

*Shirley O'Neill, center, presents the family Bible to Murray descendants Carole Confar, left, and Patricia Sharp.*

# Making a
# Present of the Past

*D*erbyshire Ancestral Research Group (DARG) is a volunteer group of about fifteen people and our aim, quite simply, is to transcribe *everything* in Derbyshire, England. We compile all record types—baptism, marriage, burial, census, will, tithe, settlement, removal orders, memorial inscriptions—anything we can find.

Our approach to transcribing memorial inscriptions is typical of our projects. We begin by making a plan of the churchyard with reference to each stone. Using this map, a group of us ventures to the cemetery on a copying expedition, carefully recording every word written on each gravestone. Then it is someone else's turn to transfer these entries to separate slips of paper which are indexed by alphabetical order. Next, all the entries are compiled into a typed list and proofread for errors. As a precaution, the final product is checked once again before being added to the collection of registers we have developed over the years. Our weekly meetings help ensure that we are always moving forward.

Although we have transcribed countless records, there are always more awaiting their turn. Each register of hundreds or even thousands of entries takes months and months to complete and I'm sure that many who observe us lurking in cemeteries and archives consider us quite mad. But each entry makes a difference to someone and every register is a labor of love.

People from all over the world contact DARG for assistance. If we can help them trace their ancestors, we happily do so. No charge is made, but if anyone is kind enough to make a donation, this money is always used to buy more supplies for the group. The more tools we have, the more people we can help. And we'd be only too happy if others elsewhere were to borrow our approach of making the past accessible and affordable. Imagine the progress we can all make if there were more of us giving the gift of roots, making a present of the past!

—*Maureen Byard, United Kingdom*

*A DARG volunteer records tombstone*
*inscriptions.*

# Rummaging for Relatives

*M*y grandfather Pritchett was born in Carthage, Missouri, and moved out West in the late 1800s. I had little knowledge of his family in the Carthage area and no known relatives there. Considerable research had produced virtually no results, so I decided to try a new tactic.

I wrote to a newspaper in Carthage asking that they publish a query in the "Letters to the Editor" section. In that query, I requested anyone with the last name of Pritchett to contact me. The only response I received was from a lady who said she was not a Pritchett and didn't know anyone by that name. What had prompted her to call was an old photograph album she had. Her father had spotted it at a rummage sale nearly fifty years earlier. Although he didn't know any of the people in the album, the book itself caught his fancy and he bought it.

This lady explained that there were about fifty photos in the album along with a remembrance card of a nine-year-old boy, Jesse Pritchett, who had accidentally shot himself back in the early 1900s. She thought that there just might be a connection. I nearly cried when she told me about this little boy because I had heard that story before. He was my grandfather's nephew.

The lady graciously mailed the photos and the card to me. I could hardly believe it when I opened the package. There were my father's aunts, uncles, and cousins. He hadn't seen some of those people for over fifty years and had no photos whatsoever of them. Now we do, and it's all due to a kind stranger in Missouri.

But the story doesn't end there. It seems this lady was as excited about my find as I was, and started telling friends and coworkers about the whole episode. One of her friends stopped her while she was telling the tale and asked, "What name did you say this gentleman was researching?"

When she replied, "Why, it's Pritchett," her friend had to blink back tears. Apparently, she had been researching Pritchetts for years and had never known about this album. Since then, I have been in contact with this fellow Pritchett researcher—of course, returning her friend's kindness by sending copies of all the pictures that had been so generously given to me. We turned out to be third cousins several times removed, and together, we have been able to construct a history of our mutual family.

I never did receive any responses from any actual Pritchetts from my query, but you won't hear me complain!

*—Jerald Thompson, Utah*

# Gone but Not Forgotten

$\mathscr{L}$t. Samuel E. Kershaw was just one of many American soldiers, pilots, and sailors who fought and died overseas during World War II. His family back in the States grieved as many other families did for servicemen who died. But in a small English village outside of London, a young boy would be affected for decades by the death of Lieutenant Kershaw, an American pilot, whose plane crashed in an open field near the village in 1945.

The young English lad was Ken Rydings. Years later in the early 1990s, that wartime scene flashed back to him when ground was broken for a new housing development on that same field outside the village. Ken made it his goal to have Lieutenant Kershaw's name made a permanent fixture of this new development. He convinced the builders to have a street named in Lieutenant Kershaw's honor and a plaque dedicated in his memory, but his primary challenge was giving the builders any personal information about Lt. Kershaw. A variety of British and American sources failed to provide any clues about the pilot's family.

*Lt. Samuel E. Kershaw.*

*Street in England named in Lt. Kershaw's honor.*

Last year, Ken was reading *Manchester Genealogical Magazine* when he spotted a query I had placed for my maiden name, which happened to be Kershaw. He took a chance that I might be related to his mystery pilot and wrote to me. I was so touched by his letter that I responded right away. I informed him there was no Samuel Kershaw in my family, but I would use resources on my side of the Atlantic to see if I could locate the pilot's family.

It took several months, but my research paid off when I succeeded in locating Samuel's stunned brother and sister. From this unexpected contact, the Kershaw family learned more about the crash than they had been told in 1945. They were only too pleased to provide information and photos of Samuel to facilitate the plaque and street naming in England, which occurred on the sixtieth anniversary of Britain's entry into the war.

I feel privileged to have been able to play a small role in this tribute. I helped Ken, and Ken helped an American family make a permanent memorial for their fallen serviceman.

—*Alice K. Luckhardt, Florida*

# PART FIVE

# Breaking the Time Barrier

*A* good genealogist strives to get past the "just the facts" mode of research—that is, just names, dates, and places—to discover what his or her ancestors were like as living, breathing people. To a non-genealogist, it may sound strange, but it is very possible to figuratively bring an ancestor back to life by following his or her trail.

"I fell in love with my great-great-grandfather" is typical of the comments committed gencalogists make when they succeed. In fact, most serious family historians find themselves drawn to a handful of ancestors, or maybe just one in particular, who call to them. These are the ancestors who want to be found, the ones who seem to find you rather than the other way around.

Learning about a great-grandfather's meritorious service in a war or a grandmother's survival in trying circumstances is often a source of pride and strength—pride in the accomplishment and strength in knowing that one comes from the same stock.

Knowing our history can make it easier to weather the storms in our own lives. Even those inevitable black sheep—the con woman, runaway dad, and other renegades—are amusing and show a family's ability to rise above circumstances. Admit it: Isn't there something appealing about knowing there's a dash of rebel blood flowing in your veins?

These tales show that even the passage of time and death itself are not strong enough to break family ties. And it seems that even when we don't know how to break this time barrier, someone on the other side often does!

# Sunbonnet Sue

$\mathcal{I}$ grew up wanting to know more about my ancestors, having been told since I was a little girl how much like my grandmother I was. I so regretted never knowing her, since she'd died shortly before my birth.

As a girl, I'd often go to the basement to practice the piano, only to divert myself to the laundry room where Mom's old cedar chest sat in a corner. It was the contents of the chest that drew me to it—treasures from times past, old pictures, baby booties, aged newspapers, even a few Confederate dollars. Mostly, I was drawn to the neatly stacked squares of white fabric, each bordered in coral and mint green, and buried underneath everything else. Sewn in the middle of each was the image of a little girl, wearing a billowed dress and big brimmed bonnet, with the fabrics and color different for each square.

I learned that my grandmother, Beulah Lenore Watson, had sewn each by hand, together with her mother, Savilla Petrie Bamber. Knowing their history, the simple squares of fabric became even more special. Lightly touching the fabric, running my fingers over each stitch, I knew other hands had once held what I held, meticulously placing each tiny stitch, and working toward the day when the quilt would be finished. Although fate decreed neither Beulah nor Savilla would live to see the completed quilt, their sewn Sunbonnet Sue squares somehow made me feel closer to them. I was certain we would have loved one another, rationalizing that anyone making a quilt full of Sunbonnet Sues must surely have loved little girls.

Through the years, other interests called me away from my infatuation with Sunbonnet Sue. Although there were occasional visits to the cedar chest, they occurred infrequently. I'd even found

*A carefully crafted Sunbonnet Sue square.*

my mother there once, looking at Sue and mentioning she'd like to finish the quilt. Unfortunately, she never did. She became very ill and this, together with my marriage, children, divorce, and then Mom's passing, caused Sunbonnet Sue to be forgotten.

It was a couple of years ago when my dad and stepmom drove to my home for a birthday celebration. Mine. A young forty-eight, or so they said. They arrived in their usual flurry, bringing smiles, love, and wisdom, and carrying a couple of wrapped gifts. When they presented the packages, I played the usual game, eyeing their shape and size, shaking them, and then concluding, "Aha! Clothes!"

As the paper fell away revealing little flowery dressed Sunbonnet Sues peeking from their tissue bed, my laughing voice went silent. My heart seemed to have jumped to my throat, or at least the lump there made me think so. I looked to Dad for answers to the question I couldn't voice. That was when Mom, my wonderful seventy-nine-year-old stepmother, told me that the quilt had been completed by some "little old ladies who get together for quilting bees."

With the quilt lovingly hugged close to me, I was, ever so briefly, that young girl at the cedar chest, discovering a love that time could not bind. It was as if my great-grandmother Bamber and my grandmother Watson were there, proud of their quilt, pleased with the beautiful finishing work of those "little old ladies," and happily approving my new gift. That was the first time I can ever recall having "cried happy."

As I tiptoe into my bedroom, my gaze strays to my bed where my two-year-old granddaughter and her mommie, my daughter, are napping, snuggled beneath multicolored Sunbonnet Sues. With feelings of love swelling up within me, I can't help but feel my grandmothers smiling, knowing three generations of grand-daughters have found warmth and comfort beneath the handiwork of their quilt. In the hush of the room and feeling the presence of more than those my eyes are resting upon, I silently whispered, "I've discovered something we each share in common—our love of daughters, granddaughters, and Sunbonnet Sue."

—*Rebecca L. Walker, Oregon*

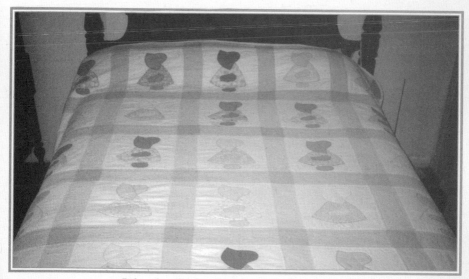

*Beloved quilt of multi-colored Sunbonnet Sues.*

# Boom-Boom Ugarrio

$\mathcal{S}$everal years ago, I hired a researcher to learn more about my husband's family. We knew from family lore that Ty's great-great-grandfather was a Cuban immigrant with the perplexing nickname of "Boom-Boom Ugarrio." His real name was Dr. Ricardo Ruiz de Ugarrio y Salvador, but we had no idea of the origin of the nickname and speculated that perhaps he had been a boxer at one time.

Most of the initial research was done at the National Archives and involved the usual census and passenger arrival records. While there, the researcher stumbled on a book in the reference room on sources in the National Archives pertaining to Latin America. She knew it was a long shot, but decided to check the index. Jackpot! An entire State Department report had been written about our Boom-Boom. But why?

The story unfolded that Boom-Boom had come to the United States in the 1880s to study to become a dentist. While here, he became an American citizen. He dearly loved his home country, however, and frequently returned to visit. On one of these trips to his homeland, he had died in a prison run by the Spanish authorities who still controlled Cuba in the late 1890s. Because he was an American citizen, the death was investigated by the State Department.

The report was to open our eyes to a piece of personal history that had been swept away in a matter of three generations. Through its seventy-five pages, we encountered a Boom-Boom who had led a double life. On the surface, he was a dentist from a well-to-do, essentially aristocratic family, but he was also a part-time freedom fighter who was reputed to have blown up trains as part of a campaign to rid his country of the Spanish. This accusation was never proved since he died just ten days after having been imprisoned, but it was the root of his nickname and the cause of the investigation which was to solve our mystery a century later.

Today, Boom-Boom is regarded as a hero in Cuba, and there's a statue of him in the Havana Harbor. I've heard it said that every family has a story, and after rediscovering the Cuban patriot in our family, I'm convinced it's true!

—Phyllis Kelley, Virginia

# Standing Tall

$\mathcal{I}$ am the granddaughter of two African-Americans, James and Lucinda East, who married in Pennsylvania in 1908 and hopped a boat one week later for South Africa. They were college educated, very idealistic and visionary, and had a dream of taking their considerable skills to Africa and "doing good works." They traveled to a rural area where they lived for eleven years from 1909 to 1920. During their time in Africa, they had four children and developed an elementary school, health clinic, farm, carpentry shop, and blacksmithery.

I have always been fascinated by their story, and that is how I became interested in genealogy. Their saga was passed down through family tales, but most of the hard evidence of their experience seemed long gone. When I started retracing their journey, I had little hope of learning much. Africa seemed such a faraway place for me to explore from my computer in California.

There is much to tell about my ten-year process of unearthing evidence, but the most remarkable part of my story follows. Wandering around the Internet, I came across a site for Fort Hare University, the school of Nelson Mandela, Desmond Tutu, and many

*James and Lucinda East.*

~ 176 ~

great African leaders. It noted that the school was founded in 1916 as an agricultural college and that the name of the first graduating student was Stanford Sonjica. This aroused my curiosity as I had heard the Sonjica name in stories about my grandparents.

After consulting a map, I realized that my grandparents had lived just a few miles from the site of Fort Hare University. On a hunch, I contacted the university to ask a vague question about agricultural development since my grandfather had written a book on his agricultural work in South Africa. I figured I might get some tidbits about his life from a kindly librarian.

To my surprise, the Dean of Agriculture, Professor Chris Igodon, responded personally. Interpreting my name as a man's, he sent an exuberant message: "Welcome Home, Brother!!!" He explained that my grandfather was a key figure in the development of the university's agricultural program. In fact, their current catalog mentions the contribution of a "Negro American, Rev. James East" as an integral part of the university's history. Imagine!

Motivated to learn more, I traveled to South Africa where I received a warm welcome at the university. While there, I was permitted access to the archives—a vaulted, dusty place closed to the public. I held my breath as we searched the cobwebby boxes and fragile files. My escort, Dr. Sean Morrow, director of Fort Hare's Department of Research, was as excited about my adventure as I was. Within minutes, we found original correspondence written in my grandfather's hand in 1915! To touch my grandfather's pale blue ink on that forgotten piece of yellowed paper in Africa brought tears to my eyes. History—my history—was suddenly alive in a way I had never imagined it could be. It was then I understood that coincidence and providence can surely work hand-in-hand. My journey to Africa, the hours on the Internet, the endless letters and phone calls, sifting though old papers, tedious documentation of dim memories—was all worthwhile. That's when I cried.

Next I visited the mission in Middledrift where my grandparents had lived and found their church was still in operation. Word spread fast that I was there, and I was greeted by *hundreds* of

*A South African welcome for the granddaughter of the Easts.*

people who came to see the African-American woman, grand-daughter of the beloved Easts. Many were children and grandchildren of my grandparents' students. I was welcomed with smiles from all, hugs from the women, African handshakes from the men, and giggles from the children. They sang beautiful songs, presented me with gifts I will cherish for the rest of my life, and even killed a sheep in my honor!

We crowded into the quaint mission church, which was decorated with an arrangement of balloons that spelled out "Welcome Bobby." Prayers were offered, Scripture was read, speeches were given. I was told repeatedly of how much the East name was loved and honored in Middledrift and points far beyond their tiny community. I was told of the many things my grandparents had accomplished that will never be forgotten. I learned that native farmers as far north as Kwazulu-Natal continue to use the "East cultivator," a special plow that was invented by my grandfather during his time in Africa. I was told of how my grandmother formed an organization of native women, encouraging them to see themselves as the daughters of kings. To this day, throughout South Africa, Baptist women commonly greet each with an expression that translates as "Hello King's Daughter!"

In response, I gave my own nervous little speech, which was translated into Xhosa for the congregates. I was once again touched by the circumstances that brought me so far from home, yet so near to my ancestors and to myself.

Prior to my research, I didn't know of my grandparents' many wonderful accomplishments. I certainly had no idea of how their deeds continue to impact lives in far-reaching corners of the world today. There is much that remains to be discovered and I'm sure I'll spend the rest of my life researching these and other leaves of the family tree. If it's true that we stand on the shoulders of our ancestors, I am blessed, for I stand tall!

—*Bobbye Dones, California*

*African women who still greet each other, "Hello King's Daughter," as encouraged by Lucinda East.*

# Dated Discovery

The Civil War enlistment papers of my great-great-grandfather, Aaron Hodges, give his birth date as 1818. His wife was born in 1809, making his 1818 birth date suspect, but still possible. It made him awfully young to be the father of the children attributed to this marriage, but try as I might, I couldn't locate any further documentation on him.

I was finally able to unravel this puzzle by making contact with a distant cousin who was fortunate enough to inherit the family Bible and written histories of the family. They provided proof that Aaron had actually been born in 1808, but better yet, they solved the mystery of why his birth date was so far off in his military papers.

One of the family histories revealed that two of Aaron's sons had enlisted in the Civil War without his permission. Concerned about their safety, he had lied about his age—claiming to be a full decade younger than he actually was—in order to be permitted to enlist. This allowed the fifty-six-year-old to be near his adventurous sons to watch over them. Thankfully, he survived the smallpox he contracted during his service.

Being the mother of a small child, it is so touching to me that a father would risk his own life, lie about his age, and take leave of his wife, just to ensure that his children would be safe. This revelation transformed a questionable birth date on a military document to a testament of the love of a father for his sons.

—*Julie K. Purdy, Washington*

# A Dash of Larceny

*M*y grandfather was a special man. He was reserved and carried himself with a sense of class. I always wondered about his past and suspected he grew up differently than we did in our middle-class neighborhood. I'm not sure if I was told not to ask him about his childhood or if I just sensed that he wasn't interested in sharing. In either case, I never asked him any questions.

After his death, I felt it was safe to ask my grandmother what she knew about his past. She said that she thought his family had been well-to-do and that his father had died when he was a young man. She never met his mother and thought that she may have died in a hospital of some sort. I was shocked to hear that she basically didn't know much more than I.

The curiosity about his past lingered and I finally decided to gather some clues. After two years of requesting birth, marriage, and death certificates, I began to see a pattern of conflicting information and became more confused.

Then a breakthrough. While searching on line, I found a connection to my grandfather's first cousin. She never knew my grandfather, but had heard many stories of his mother. Her mother told her that my great-grandmother was a high-society lady in San Francisco, but thought she may have been in some trouble with the law.

Now my interest was soaring, so I decided to do a newspaper search to see if I could learn more. I went to the library and was guided to newspaper records for the San Francisco area. Looking for my great-grandmother's name, Dorothy Hammell, I came up blank, but I did find numerous listings for a Barbette Hammel. Could they be the same woman?

# Barbette, Planning Writing Career, Enters San Quentin

Barbette Hammel (left) leaving Alameda Jail with Deputy Sheriff Pauline Walker.

'It's Lovely Old Place; I'll Be Happy There,' She Says on First View of Penitentiary

*February 21, 1929* San Francisco Chronicle *clipping about the infamous Barbette.*

Pulling the actual articles, the first entry I found for Barbette contained a picture of a stunning-looking woman wearing a suit edged in fur. The headline read, "Beauty Flees S.F. Fraud Net—Barbette Hammel Hunted on Jewel Theft Warrant—S.F. Beauty Suspected of $100,000 Fraud Plot in Bad Check Deals." This was certainly interesting! I went to the next article and the next until I came upon one that gave my great-grandfather's name as her husband. I remember feeling exhilarated that I had found her and at the same time feeling quite sad when I realized that this was my grandfather's mother. Now I knew why he never shared his past.

Since then, I have continued to gather articles on my great-grandmother. At last count, I had over one hundred that span a period of almost forty years.

From the information I found, I pieced together a magnificent tale. Her story is best summed up by a March 1947 *San Francisco Chronicle* article that reads:

*Will you ever forget Barbette Hammel? Now there was a woman with chic, dash and imagination to say nothing of larceny. There was nothing bush league about Barbette. Big or small, she bilked 'em all. With money she fast talked out of others, she opened a swank beauty salon on Powell called Salon Barbette, promoted The Hammel School for Subnormal Children, and sold a bill of goods on The Hammel Vegetable Concession—an outfit to sell shelled peas to fancy hotels and restaurants . . .*

*The cops called her "the cleverest confidence woman to work here in years." The newspapers couldn't make up their minds whether she was Lady Wallingford, The Siren of Swindle, or The Female Ponzi. A jury in Superior Court eventually decided she was just plain guilty.*

*Pretty Barbette entered San Quentin with a flourish worthy of Hildegarde. She looked around and sighed, "It's such a lovely old place."*

*Yes, whatever happened to Barbette Hammel?*

You can be sure that this last question is one her great-granddaughter will answer!

—*Lori Hammell-Davis, California*

# Island of Tears

$\mathcal{I}$n looking for the passenger ship arrival records for all of my father's family, I began a search for my great-aunt Catharina (née Horn) Spiegel and her three daughters who arrived from Hungary in the early part of this century. I knew that Catharina and her three daughters –Margaret, Elizabetha, and Catharina—had arrived in New York in late November 1910.

During a research trip to the National Archives Regional Branch, I looked for "Spiegel" and located the ship. A search of the ship's passenger arrival records uncovered the listing of Catharina and her three daughters. As was my practice, although I had never turned up anything by doing so, I then turned to the end of the list to review the list of detainees. This list shows those persons who were detained on Ellis Island while waiting to learn their fate as to whether or not they would be allowed entrance into the United States. Surprisingly, I found Catharina's three daughters listed there. This meant there was a story and I couldn't wait to go home and call my cousin Maria, Catharina Speigel's granddaughter.

That night at home, while waiting for my cousin to return my phone call, I read and reread the two photocopies of the passenger list and the list of detainees wondering what story they held. So excited was I on finding the list of detainees that I ignored the obvious answer that lay before me. But at long last, my mind finally registered the surprising piece of information on the list that I had overlooked. Catharina Spiegel had a fourth daughter, Apollonia, only fifteen months old!

In the entry next to her name it looked as if someone had written the words "died December 3, 1910." Finally after what seemed like years, my cousin Maria returned my call and I told her that I had discovered Apollonia. After a long silence, Maria began

*Cathy Horn stands at Apollonia's recently located
burial site.*

to speak, saying that she had vague recollections of hearing her
mother and grandmother discussing Ellis Island, a baby who died
there, and their longing to know where the baby was buried. Maria
said that her own mother and two aunts had remained on Ellis
Island for several days, alone and frightened children in a foreign
country without their mother. Maria also recalled the story that her
grandmother and baby were taken to a hospital where they were
separated. After a few days, her grandmother was told that the baby
had died. So Catharina Spiegel, upon her release from the hospital,
continued on to Ellis Island to pick up her three other daughters.
Together, they traveled to Pennsylvania where she and her husband
lived until their deaths, never knowing what happened to their
baby, Apollonia.

During another research trip to the New York City Municipal
Archives, my search of the death records for Richmond County,
more commonly known as Staten Island, turned up Apollonia's
death record. She and her mother had stayed at the Hospital for
Contagious Diseases on Hoffman Island, a small island located off
of Staten Island at the entrance to New York Harbor. According to
the death certificate, Apollonia died ten days after the ship arrived in

| | | |
|---|---|---|
| Myer Spack | Antonio Speziali | Andrew and Athena Toutounzi |
| Frank and Lucia Spada | Henry and Mary Wood Spice | Spyrides |
| The Michele Spada Family | Pauline Spicer | Theodora Andriopoulos Spyros |
| Antonio Spadaccini | Paul Spiciarich | The Peter A. Squadrito Family |
| Cesaria Manfredi Spadaccini | John Spicola | Paul Squarcia |
| The Dominick Spadafora Family | Mary LaGaipa Spicola | Helen Carpentieri Squeo |
| Giuseppe Spadafora | The Vincent Spicuzza Family | Francesco Squicciarini |
| Rosa DeVuono Spadafora | Joseph Spidalieri | Isabel Azzolini Squicciarini |
| Antonio G. B. Spadafore | Apollonia Spiegel | Luigi and Bedelia Squillante |
| John and Rosa Spadafore | Flora H. Spiegel | Amalia Squitieri |
| Carmelo Spadaro | Herbert P. Spiegel | The Antonio Squitieri Family |
| Joseph and Millie Spadaro | Joseph Spiegel | Luigi Squitieri |
| Theresa Frontino Spadaro | Joseph David and Gussie Posin | Isaac R. Seager |
| Caterina Spadea | Spiegel | Blazo Sredanovic |
| Vincenzo Spadea | Murray Spiegel | The Emanuela and Marija Sre |
| | Nellie Kurtzman Spiegel | Family |
| | | George and Mary Matias Srn |
| | | John Seneca |

*Apollonia Spiegel's memory lives on through the Wall of Honor at Ellis Island.*

New York. A review of the detainee listing showed that her sisters had remained alone on Ellis Island for seven days. Based on the difference between Apollonia's death date and day her sisters left Ellis Island, it appears that Apollonia may still have been alive when her mother left the hospital. However, with the number of fatal diseases listed on the death certificate, her death was probably considered imminent. And so fifteen-month-old Apollonia died alone in a foreign county without her mother or her family.

I next learned that the Edward Scully Funeral Home held the contract during the early part of this century for burials for anyone who died en route to Ellis Island. Their name is on Apollonia's death certificate which also shows that she was buried in Mt. Olivet Cemetery, in Queens County, New York. On writing to the cemetery, I received a letter confirming that she is buried there in an unmarked grave and a map showing the location within the cemetery where her body was interred.

After being lost to her family for eighty-three years and almost lost to memory, fifteen-month-old Apollonia had finally been found. Although she never landed on Ellis Island, known both as a gateway to America and an island of tears, her name will be remembered on the Wall of Honor at Ellis Island. Apollonia will also remain in our hearts as well as our family history and will never be forgotten again.

—*Cathy Horn, New York*

# Apron Strings

*M*y great-great-grandmother, Berit Gandrud, was born in Norway in 1832. By 1866, she was already a widow with three children and pregnant with her fourth. Living in a second home on her father's farm, Vesle Gandrud, she endured the deaths of her father and daughter. Perhaps to escape the memories, Berit decided to take her remaining family to America to join her brothers in Minnesota.

Over the years, her descendants scattered throughout Minnesota and Canada, but one of her granddaughters, Louise, was determined to keep the family spirit alive.

Louise shared the old stories and traditions with her own children, and passed on to her daughter Verna one of the few remaining family heirlooms—an apron that her grandmother Berit had worn in Norway on special occasions.

Seeking to find out more about my family, I contacted Pete Gandrud, a fellow roots-seeker who turned out to be my third cousin. He had completed extensive family research, and even traveled to the family home in Norway. We exchanged photos, and one among the

*Wearing her apron, Berit Gandrud, left, poses with her sister Randi in 1850s Norway.*

*Four generations of Berit's descendants with her apron: (L-R) Megan Ham, Kayle Ham, Myrna Varley and Myra Chapman.*

batch that Peter sent caught me by surprise. It was of my great-great-grandmother Berit, taken in Norway when she was a girl! I immediately sent a copy to Verna. She recognized Berit, but more important, she recognized what Berit was wearing—the very same apron that had been given to her for safekeeping.

That apron, which I had been unaware of until that time, has survived more than 150 years. Berit may have worn it at her wedding. It may have been stuffed in a steamer trunk bound for America, in the hope that there would be special events to come, occasions important enough to wear it. Berit may even have been wearing the apron as she bid good-bye to her family and homeland and headed for New York. How incredible it was to see and hold it today. The colors are amazingly vivid, not faded at all—just as the spirit that seems to be woven into it.

Out of all the personal belongings that could have been handed down through the generations, it was the apron that was saved. And out of all the family treasures that Peter Gandrud might have found, it was the photograph of Berit wearing that apron. In a letter to Peter I wrote, "I didn't even know that you existed until a few months ago. Out of all the space—physical and otherwise—

between you and me, we found each other, you sent me a photo, I sent it to Verna, and the story became a full circle."

I believed that the story had indeed rounded into a complete circle at that point, but I was in for another surprise. Hanging in the National Gallery in Oslo, Norway, is a famous depiction of a woman sitting at a loom, weaving fabric. The painting, *Kone i vevstol*, was created in 1874 by one of Norway's most revered artists, Adolph Tidemand. About a year after I discovered Berit's apron, I found out that Tidemand painted the portrait at Berit's former home, Vesle Gandrud. According to historians, the woman in the picture is Berit's sister Live.

The painting is truly a moment in time—in Berit's time. A hutch with a large mixing bowl, a sunlit window, an open door adorned in dramatic carved design, the massive loom—a glimpse of what Berit would want to share with us. With Live's back to the viewer, it isn't possible to see what she was wearing, but I like to believe it was another fine apron that found its way into the appreciative hands of *her* descendants.

—*Carin Van Vooren, California*

# Surveying across the Centuries

$\mathcal{M}$y parents grew up in the towns that had been long associated with their families, one in central and the other in southwestern Pennsylvania. Upon marriage, they relocated to upstate New York, thus severing the connections to those communities for their children.

After college, I decided to settle not in my parents' hometowns, but on the other side of Pennsylvania, in Philadelphia. My attraction, I rationalized, was its "European city" quality. As a landscape architect, I got to know the region well. In particular, I spent a lot of time in Bristol Borough, a small community on the Delaware River. Our firm had been its planning consultants for years, and I had done much survey work and historical research.

In spite of the problems that face Philadelphia, I have always loved it and felt that I belonged here. Last year, in my twenty-third year in the city, I finally decided to seek out my roots. In just a matter of days, I found a connection to my mother's side on a Quaker genealogy Web site and was able to trace the family back to the 1500s in Germany. I hadn't even known we were Quaker!

I was amazed to discover that the place they first came to in America was Philadelphia, and remnants of their homes, churches, and burial grounds are all within a half mile of my house! The real surprise, however, was learning that my first ancestor to arrive in this country in 1685 was a surveyor, and had lived in and surveyed Bristol Borough, a new town at the time. So he and I had measured the same things in the same place about three hundred years apart! No wonder I have such a sense of belonging here. Now I suspect that my choices of hometown and work were not so much "rational" as inevitable!

—*Kathy Kelly, Pennsylvania*

# The Picture on the Wall

$\mathcal{I}$ had known very little about my half sister who died in 1926. Many times, for over fifty years, I had wondered about her. My mother spoke of her only once during all those years—I'm sure because it was so painful and "a closed book."

Mother had always kept a picture of a little girl on her bedroom wall, and I knew in my heart this was my half sister. A couple of times I asked mother who this child was, but her only reply would be, "Oh, that's a friend's baby."

After Mother passed away in 1996 at the age of ninety-two, I was packing up some of her things and suddenly realized that now I could actually look closely at this little face without a name, and even touch the picture on the wall. I carefully took the picture down and removed it from the frame. There was something written on the back of the picture—my mother's previous married name and an address—a starting place!

After I retired in 1998, I decided it was time to pursue the matter, but the question was where

*The mysterious picture on the wall.*

to start. My daughter sent e-mails to several people with the last name we were looking for, and whose profiles stated an interest in genealogy. We both thought finding anyone connected to our unknown baby was about as likely as winning the lottery, but find them she did! Within a few days a man wrote back saying his wife's uncle had been married to a woman with my mother's name, and there was a child who died in 1926. He gave us the phone number of his wife's only remaining aunt.

The next day, with trembling hands, I dialed the woman's phone number. I told her who I was and what I was searching for. She said, "Oh yes, I can give you the name of the child and the exact date of death." I thanked her profusely and hung up.

My daughter and I then went to the genealogy department at the Tacoma Library and began searching the Washington Death Index. Within minutes we found her. I now had the death certificate number and could send to Olympia for the death certificate itself. The waiting was almost unbearable, but within a few days many of the pieces of the puzzle had fallen into place—her name, parents' names, date of birth, cause of death, and where she was buried. She is buried in a mausoleum less than five miles from where I have lived almost all of my life.

Now, seventy-three years after the death of this precious little angel who was only fourteen months old when she died, I finally know something about my half sister. I have visited the mausoleum several times and placed a vase of artificial pink rosebuds and a little teddy bear on the shelf. Thanks to people with an interest in family history and the miracle of the Internet, there is some closure to the mystery of the picture on the wall.

—*Beverly Knoll, Washington*

# Robert's Legacy

$\mathcal{G}$enealogy is usually fun. Going through musty old books in the courthouse, running microfilm through the reader, walking through cemeteries, and taking photos are all my idea of a good time. Each year, we devote some time to traveling in our RV to places where our ancestors lived. We like to spend a week, sometimes two if the picking is good.

One of these trips found us in the old Fulton County Courthouse in New York. Each time we stumbled on the surname we were researching, we were sent off in another direction. Soon the table was full of references of books, census and cemetery records, and other documents. We went through each one and transferred all the information into our files and made copies. Then we went back in the RV and reviewed our work in dismay. All of this information, but no real connection to the family.

After dinner, a deep discussion ensued. We had set aside two weeks for this search in New York. What was going wrong? A good part of the allotted time had elapsed with no results. Despair was setting in. Then we remembered who we were looking for—the ancestor who had come from Scotland in 1787. Instead of using a shotgun approach and finding many slivers of information about all sorts of people, perhaps a rifle aimed directly at the one central name would work better. The key was to find him: Robert Stewart.

The next day we traveled to the new Fulton County Courthouse and headed directly to the Probate Court Office. The counties were split in 1837 and we weren't sure when Robert had died. We opted to start with the old county records and found Robert's will in the index in fairly short order. After being sent to the basement to dusty but carefully labeled file cabinets, I came up triumphant clutching several envelopes filled with documents. I was practically jumping around with impatience as I waited for them to be copied. When I had the

*Excerpt from Robert Stewart's will.*

precious copies, I took them back to the RV and looked through them over lunch. Comparing the will with my earlier research, it was clear that I had the right man.

The will itself was a revelation not only of the structure of the family, but also of the personality of the man himself. I was touched that he had taken pains to provide for even the smallest needs of his wife, Jane, after his death:

> . . . *my said son, William, provide a horse and waggon for his said mother to carry her to meeting and to any other place where she desires to go . . . as much firewood as she shall need, to be brought to her chopped and left at the door, ready for her use*

By today's standards, these kinds of "privileges" might seem rather minuscule, but in the early 1800s, they reflected a man who deeply loved the wife who had borne him twelve children and left all that was familiar to her to venture to the New World with him.

From other details in the will, we were able to find the location of Robert Stewart's old homestead in the small village of Sammonsville. Even today, it is still known as the Stewart Farm, though now owned by another family. As I stood there looking at the remaining foundation and the old road overgrown with trees, I knew that this was where Robert and Jane's American legacy was launched. I savored the view with a palpitating heart, and then taped it so that others in my family could experience the same sensation. Our research effort had been tremendously successful. I had met my great-great-great-grandfather, Robert Stewart.

—*Bruce and Mary Kay Stewart, Arizona*

# Finding My Father

$\mathscr{I}$ was born in January 1945, just three months before my father was killed in an explosion in Germany. A V-Mail letter from my father, dated February 15, 1945, was taped to my baby book:

> Dear Susan,
> Yours is a pretty good family as families run. Your dad is a bit on the off side. Your mother is the most wonderful person I've ever known. I've always marveled at my great good fortune to have loved her and been loved by her. If you will follow her dictates and examples, you may expect to meet life in the best possible way, and your path will always be the right one. For me, adhere to a belief in tolerance, a genuine liking for others, and always give to life to the fullest.
> Your father,
> Dave

This was all I ever knew of my father. My mother eventually remarried and I became one of nine siblings. I queried my mother about my father, but her recollections were hazy. In 1992— nearing my fiftieth birthday and the fiftieth anniversary of my father's

*Susan several years after she received her father's V-mail letter.*

death—I felt the need to fill the void. A few calls led me to the American WWII Orphans Network* which, in turn, told me how to get my father's service records.

The records—singed on the edges from a fire that struck the St. Louis repository—arrived and in two minutes, revealed more about my father than I had ever known. He was five-foot-eleven and 140 pounds. He had majored in history at Carleton College in Minnesota and rode and trained horses. He listed sailing and swimming as sports he was proficient in. I grew up sailing, never imagining he'd sailed the same lake several decades earlier. When he died, his possessions included a Bible, twenty pairs of socks, and a wallet with $38.67.

A letter I found among the records dated January 1951 stated that an investigation had failed to reveal a "grave at which to pay homage." It seemed shameful that there is no grave, no final spot that belongs to my father, to his family.

Encouraged by these initial results, I worked up the courage to contact members of my father's battalion. One man led to another, and I slowly learned about the circumstances surrounding his death. I was relieved to find that he was respected and well liked by the men who served with him.

Still, this wasn't enough, so I decided to go to Europe to follow the battalion's route across France, Belgium, and Germany. With the help of a local policeman, details from the investigation of my father's death, and special maps, my husband and I drove down a neglected road and eventually came to a place surrounded by barbed wire. Below us was a bowl-shaped crater, where the earth had been carved out.

Lt. David Johnson, Susan's father.

I sat down cross-legged and looked into the crater at the spot where my father died. I read a poem, and my husband said a prayer. I talked with my daddy for the first time. I told him that I love him. I told him about his grandchildren and daughter-in-law. I told him about all the people who helped me find him.

My eyes were drawn to a white birch tree on the far hill, which had become radiantly beautiful. A white-gold light shone from the center of it. Heaven had opened. My father was all right.

When I returned to America, I called the American Battle Monuments Commission to arrange for a marker for my father. On July 28, 1997, my father finally got his long overdue funeral— with full ceremony—at Arlington National Cemetery. I thought I should feel sad, but I felt triumphant walking down the road behind the soldiers, with my husband and two children beside me. My father is no longer lost "somewhere in Germany." In an odd way, he has come home.

—*Dr. Susan Hadler, Washington, D.C.*

* To learn more about AWON, the American WWII Orphans Network, go to www.awon.org or contact 910 Princess Anne St., Suite 304, Fredericksburg, Virginia 22401 (AWON@aol.com).

*The V-mail letter sent to Susan from her father.*

# Just What I Wanted

*My grandmother inspired my love for genealogy. She shared her favorite childhood memories and put names to the faces in the ancient photos that cluttered her drawers. Grandma would have loved cyberspace, but nothing takes the place of visiting the areas that your ancestors once walked. It is in her memory that I relate a story she wrote around 1944:*

On a motor trip through New England, my husband reluctantly consented to help me check some libraries for family information I hoped would be there. This particular day we were settled in a small one that had single reading desks lined up in school-like rows.

He decided that it might save time if I'd find the books, then bring them back for him to copy down the information. This had gone on for some time, although unhappily the results were meager. Finally he said, "Hadn't we better get on the road? I'd like to get to a good motel before dark."

"Just a half hour longer," I begged. "I still think I can find what I need."

He grudgingly agreed and I rushed back to check books as fast as I could. Time was passing much too quickly. As the half hour approached and passed by, I didn't dare look in my husband's direction, fearing that it would remind him of our bargain. I was getting frustrated, then at last I found the book. With a quick check of the index and a glance at the first few pages, I hurried back with my find.

It was a large book, but I got it safely down on the desk while still keeping my place.

Hoping to mollify him, I put my arm around his shoulder and leaned down to whisper in his ear, "Darling, thank you so much for waiting. I've found just what I wanted."

"Y-you h-have?" a frightened, unfamiliar voice answered. Looking up quickly, I saw my impatient husband waiting at the door. I was draped around the shoulders of a stranger.

*—Elouise Jenness Leonard (1904–1991),*
*shared in loving memory by her granddaughter,*
*Judy Leonard Bruckner, Missouri*

# Mistaken Identity

*I*n 1936, my mother, now deceased, wrote a letter to the government trying to determine what had happened to her great-grandfather. She received a response saying that James Beatty enlisted in the Union Army in 1861 in Ohio and served as a private. He had been wounded in the left hip, was discharged in 1865 in Arkansas, and died in a home for veterans in 1912.

For years, my family believed this to be fact. By chance last summer, my daughter-in-law had to go to Ohio on business. I went along to baby-sit. During that time, I was able to squeeze in just one hour at the Ohio State Archives before my newborn granddaughter insisted on leaving. The only task I managed to accomplish was getting the death certificate for James Beatty. As I checked it on my return trip to Illinois, I realized that the James Beatty referred to in the 1936 correspondence was not really my great-great-grandfather. He had the wrong wife and children.

After getting over the initial surprise, I wrote to the National Archives to obtain Civil War records for the *right* James Beatty. I was gratified to find my great-great-grandfather's papers and get a peek into his life through the assorted affidavits filed by his friends in support of his petition for a pension.

But what made the experience even more special was the revelation that *my* James Beatty had an unclaimed Civil War medal! Equipped with the new information from the correct file and proof that I was a direct descendant, I was able to apply to the state of West Virginia for the medal. It arrived on the first birthday of James's fourth great-granddaughter, my protesting companion at the Ohio State Archives, so we had double reason to celebrate!

*James Beatty's previously unclaimed
Civil War medal.*

Had this medal been claimed in the 1860s, it surely would have been lost during the intervening generations. We are grateful that it was waiting for his descendants all of these years, and knowing from his records the hardships that James and his family endured as a result of his Civil War service makes it all the more meaningful. You can be sure that this treasured memento that came to us through an incident of mistaken identity will be carefully guarded and cherished by future generations.

—*Karen Meng, Illinois*

# Pass to Freedom

One afternoon in the early 1970s, my mother was clearing out her dresser drawers as part of her spring cleaning. Our son was sitting on the floor beside her examining all her treasures, ready to put them in his cache for future perusal along with his baseball cards and comic books. In the midst of her possessions, he spied a small piece of white sackcloth, a little larger than a dollar bill, with "Elizabeth Welb born in Neuse River" written on it and the word "FREE" printed in large, bold letters. He asked Gram about it, and the story began to unfold.

Elizabeth Welb was born around 1805 in North Carolina. She had been born into slavery and this scrap of cloth was the document indicating that a former slave had been set free. It was required to be in their possession at all times. The pass had been carefully shepherded through generation after generation in my family, but until then, I had no idea this piece of fabric existed.

I remember my first awareness of my great-great-great-grandmother's Pass to Freedom, as we call it, bringing with it a feeling of profound sadness, coupled with an overwhelming calm. It was a time for deep reflection knowing that I was actually touching the same FREE pass that she was forced to wear for protection and survival, lest she be forced back into slavery by some unscrupulous fiend. It was my turn to tap into the pain that had been experienced by ancestors of each generation since hers.

My feelings are like a kaleidoscope each time I touch or speak about this document. My imagination soars as I place myself in her time before she was issued this pass. My thoughts are haunted when I think of the indignities she was forced to suffer. Did she know the love and gentle touch of a family or was she just another pickaninny on Massa's plantation? How old was she when she was given the pass? Under what circumstances did she receive her freedom? We assume Welb was the name of the plantation owner who gave her freedom, but I wonder who named her Elizabeth.

The Pass to Freedom was copied to a medal and used in the 1976 Bicentennial, and the document itself toured the country. I had an opportunity to travel displaying the pass and found many people like myself who had never seen such a document. There was no mention of this type of document in schoolbooks when I was a youngster and I don't believe it has changed as of this writing. I intend to seek opportunities to fill this gap in our historical awareness with Elizabeth's Pass to Freedom before I give it to her great-great-great-great-granddaughter.

—*E. Louise Peek Allen, Arizona*

*Elizabeth Welb's "FREE" pass set against a backdrop of the Neuse River.*

# Sacred Memories

$\mathscr{M}$y wife, through family tragedy, lost virtually everything related to her family, except cherished memories. She had perhaps two photos of her now-deceased parents. I decided as a Christmas present a few years ago that I would try to find out about her family tree.

Since I was new to genealogical research at the time, I began by collecting information on how to conduct such research and came up with the usual recommendations—that is, vital records, church records, and so forth. I at least had the advantage of knowing that her mother's family had been in San Francisco for three generations.

In the course of my research, I learned that my wife's mother and grandmother had attended Dominican, at that time a Catholic women's college in San Rafael, California. In an effort to get a copy of my wife's mother's grades, I contacted the nuns of Dominican College and told them of my attempt to collect as much family history as I could to replace all that had been destroyed. The nun I talked with put me in touch with the college's archivist who looked up both women. As my wife's grandmother graduated in 1914 (no small feat for a woman at that time), there was little information on her, but the unexpected gold mine lay ahead regarding my wife's mother.

For some reason, Marie Welch, my wife's mother, had made a complete scrapbook of her college years and left it at the school. Still in safe keeping at the college was a large, leather-bound album full of notes, letters, pictures, remembrances, and drawings. Within its pages, invitations to dances, parties, and weddings still mingled with a lingering hint of perfume. It was a find beyond expectation and the nuns generously gave me this treasure they had been holding for over fifty years.

When my wife opened the book on Christmas and realized what it was, all she could do was cry tears of joy. I'm sure wherever her mother was, she did the same. After this experience, would you be surprised to hear that I am absolutely hooked on family research?

—*Jeff Lintner, California*

# A Forgotten Treasure

$\mathscr{I}$t is the early 1900s. A blond teenager with large blue eyes that are dancing with excitement looks to the front where a lady stands. She is ready to draw a name, and he hopes that he will be the lucky one. He is!

My grandparents, Thomas and Grace Scott Splan, passed away in the 1950s. Their belongings were divided among their five children. Among other items from her parents' home, my mother, Frances Splan Peltier, received two quilts. The quilts had been heavily used and were beginning to show wear.

My mother sewed the quilts inside a new red-and-blue-plaid covering. The new quilt was used during our family camping trips as a mat, at home as a quilt when we were cold, and as extra bedding when company visited. My brother and I referred to it as the "red quilt." It was always special to us because it was heavy, warm, and cuddly. We never knew that there were other quilts inside.

By the 1970s, the plaid quilt cover my mother had made began to wear out and she decided to make a new covering. After removing the red covering and knowing of my interest in genealogy, my mother decided not to recover the two quilts. Instead she called to ask if I would like one of the quilts that had been sewn inside. As the red quilt had been a part of my childhood I said, "Of course." Little did I know that the quilt I was to receive was a genealogical treasure!

In 1910, Chas Osborn was the governor of Michigan, and there was a small community called Parkersville, located in Michigan's Upper Peninsula. Today that community no longer exists. However, the community lives on through the quilt I received.

The quilt was originally created by the members of a small rural church in Parkersville as a fundraiser in the early 1900s.

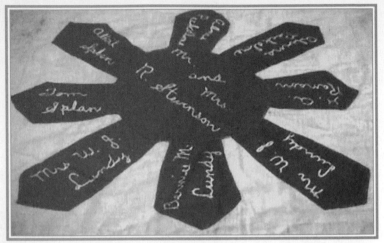

*A square of Parkersville, Michigan names from the rediscovered quilt.*

The members of the church made the quilt, which has a white muslin background with forty-two flowers, one on each quilt block. Each flower has multiple petals. On each center and petal the quilters stitched their names, and those of their husbands and children. There are over four hundred individuals listed on the quilt.

When the quilt was completed, a raffle was held. The blond teenager with the dancing eyes who won the quilt was my grandfather. To date its age, I used the genealogical information stitched on the quilt itself and was able to ascertain that it was completed after 1910 and before 1914.

Most of the adults listed on the quilt were born in Ontario of the 1850s and 1860s. It has been a remarkable adventure trying to track them down. I am in the process of trying to find out about the lives of the community and its members, and there is much more that can be learned from the quilt. It truly is a treasure and a remarkable history for families with Parkerville roots.

—*Sandy Peltier Caden, Michigan*

# PART SIX

# What Were the Odds?

*H*ave you ever found yourself thousands of miles from home, only to come face-to-face with a neighbor, a high school buddy, or someone you served with in the military decades ago?

It takes a moment or two to place the person because they're out of context, but then you greet each other and inevitably wonder out loud what the odds are that you would run into each other this way.

There's a genealogical equivalent to this situation and it happens with surprising regularity. Many avid family history buffs have made some of their most significant discoveries against ridiculous odds. They have an uncanny ability to be in the right place at the right time. They trip across the information they're seeking in the most unexpected ways. And they will spot the pivotal clue that literally flashes before their eyes for a brief moment or two.

If genealogists were gamblers, they'd be the kind you'd want to hang out with in the hope that some of their luck would rub off on you. Here's just a small sample of roots-seekers beating the odds.

# A Really Good Friday

*A*s I searched the records of Jackson County, Minnesota, I was unable to find the birth record of a sibling of my grandmother. According to my great-grandfather's obituary, the child had died in infancy. I felt great disappointment, as I had never known about this missing child and wanted to learn more about her.

Needing to take a break from the dusty volumes, my daughter and I headed to the far corner of the county to see the graves of great-great-grandparents whose location we discovered in the records. There, in an old cemetery behind the now newer church, were the graves of my great-great-grandparents, Ludwig Pallas and Karolina Adler Pallas. Beside them, with a hard-to-read head-stone, was what appeared to be the grave of this little great-aunt whom I never knew.

This was an unexpected discovery, but almost more surprising was the fact that the church office was open. I thought this was odd since it was the afternoon of Good Friday, but didn't question my good fortune. The lady there kindly explained that the records for the cemetery were with the church elders. All she had was an old ledger-type book. She opened it to emphasize her words, and pointed to a random entry, explaining, "See, it's all in German."

Her finger pointed to the entry for Karolina Marie Thompson, the very child for whom we searched! There were her dates of birth and death, along with verification of her parents' names. Because she had died the same day she was born, her birth had never been recorded in the county's civil records.

My final piece of good luck? The reason the church was open on Good Friday was because they were having a copy machine delivered. The man had just finished installing and setting it up as I wandered in. They tested the copy machine for me by running copies of the entries for my records!

—*Diane Wrightsman Tavoian, Texas*

# Split-Second Timing

$\mathscr{M}$y great-great-grandfather, William N. Jones, had been missing for about 130 years. Family lore had it that he and a group of men marched off to join the Civil War and were never heard from again. I took up the search in archives, books, and local records, but he was not to be found. His fate remained a question mark to his many descendants.

Like so many people, my husband and I were mesmerized by the popular *Civil War* documentary in the early 1990s. We sat watching one evening when something caught my eye in the briefest of segments. It was a mortality list for a prison. Fortunately, my husband had taped the episode so we froze the screen and struggled to read the names on the blurry page. Sure enough—the page contained the name of my missing soldier!

We backtracked from the PBS segment, not even knowing which prison it represented, to mortality records at the archives. Within minutes, we had the record of my great-great-grandfather's last known whereabouts! The sad news was that Sergeant Jones had died as a prisoner of war at Camp Chase, Ohio, in 1865. He probably didn't even know that he had left his children orphaned as his wife had predeceased him just a few months earlier.

Armed with this new information, we rerequested his service records, which had apparently been misfiled. Having at least a few facts about his death and military service made it possible at last to find the misplaced records.

We learned that he had traveled around in several states and participated in many battles, but was ultimately captured within a half mile of the very archives that contained his mortality records. His records had been accidentally blended into the file of William *H.* Jones, a deserter. In the old handwriting, the middle initials

"N" and "H" looked very similar, thus creating the problem that was to take us so long to solve. A note was inserted in the deserter's records in 1894 stating that the government knew that my ancestor's records were in the incorrect file, but they were not correcting them. So it was to take almost another hundred years before a split-second frame in a television documentary would provide the key to unlock this family mystery and give my great-great-grandfather, William N. Jones, back to his family.

—*Nanette Jones Reepe, Georgia*

# Home Again

$\mathscr{I}$ knew that my grandmother was originally from Bedford, Pennsylvania, but having grown up in another part of the state, and then moving to the Washington, D.C., area, I had never been to Bedford. My wife and I decided to visit to see what information we could dig up about my grandmother's family. We had a Chamber of Commerce booklet from Bedford, so we picked a place to stay from that booklet—a bed-and-breakfast right in town, near the courthouse and county historical society.

We had a very pleasant trip and stay at the old house in downtown Bedford. When we got home, I took another look at the Chamber of Commerce brochure and noticed there was a map of Bedford that showed all of the historic buildings, as well as their names and brief histories. It caught my attention that one house was referred to as the "Shuck House." I was excited, since one of the new surnames I had discovered in my ancestry during the trip was Shuck.

Looking more closely at the map, I saw that this Shuck house was near the B&B we stayed in—in fact, *it was that very house*. I ultimately learned that the

*Portrait of Daniel Shuck (1786-1845).*

*The Bedford House Bed & Breakfast, formerly known as the "Shuck House"*
*in Bedford, Pennsylvania.*

house we had stayed in on our first trip to Bedford had been owned by my ancestors from the early 1800s until the 1950s!

The story doesn't end here, though. Over time, we became friends with the owners of the B&B, a transplanted New England couple. When they bought the house next to the B&B to expand the business, they found old glass-plate photo negatives in the attic. Lo and behold, that house was also owned by the Shucks, and by correlating information on the negatives with census records, I identified the subjects of the pictures as my ancestors, Samuel and Annie Shuck and their three daughters. As nearly as I can tell, most of the photos—which turned out perfectly when developed—are from the 1870s. Also in the attic were record books from the family businesses, which included a tannery and general merchandise, plus a stack of handbills advertising that Samuel Shuck was selling some land. Since he died in 1889, I know the handbills must be at least 110 years old.

Even more amazing, the 1870s Shucks had been concerned enough about the family's posterity to have a photograph made of a portrait of Daniel Shuck—my great-great-great-great-grandfather who was born in 1786! What a find! And all because of the B&B we picked out of a brochure!

—*Greg Kleist, Maryland*

# Small World

About four years ago, I became interested in genealogy and started tracing various relatives. One of the relatives I was most interested in was my maternal grandfather. Although he passed away in 1965, we had lived with him when I was young and I felt a close kinship with him. Unfortunately, everyone who knew him had also passed on. I knew the name of the town he came from in Ireland—Templeglantine in County Limerick—but was unable to locate it on any available maps. I even had business colleagues in Ireland try to locate the town to no avail.

It seems that many small towns in rural Ireland consist of only a church and a few farms and don't necessarily appear on maps. While towns and townlands are not exactly the same thing, the fact that there are approximately sixty-four thousand townlands gives an idea of how challenging my search was to be. I was very frustrated as I couldn't locate Templeglantine anywhere, and without being able to locate it, my search was dead-ended.

After about a year of frustration, I found myself in Dubai in the United Arab Emirates on a business trip. One night there was a large dinner with roughly one thousand in attendance. I happened to arrive late and found my seat occupied. Rather than displace the person, I located a vacant seat at another table and sat down. After introducing myself to my tablemates, I discovered one of them had an Irish accent. I couldn't resist the temptation and proceeded to tell him about my thwarted attempts to find my grandfather's town. He advised me that this was not uncommon as towns this small often change their names or are absorbed into other towns. Sometimes they just cease to exist.

"By the way," he said, "what is the name of the town you're interested in?" Imagine our mutual shock when I learned he had been born in Templeglantine and he learned that this was the tiny town I was seeking! He then told me all about the town and how to obtain data from the local parish priest. So I finally visited Templeglantine where I met my Limerick cousins after a slight detour through the Middle East!

—*John Flynn, Illinois*

# Blind Luck
# Can Lead You Home

*W*hen I was thirteen, my father received an appointment for a sabbatical in Uppsala, Sweden, so our family lived there for about a year. Several months into our stay, we took a road trip to Trondheim, Norway, the place from which my father's grandparents had emigrated in the 1890s. All he knew about his grandparents was that their names were Andrew Aune and Kari Hegstad.

We stopped in villages along the way and inquired at newspaper offices and stores with the name Aune on the door. We were very naive about how to find our roots, and had no idea how wildly common the name Aune is in Norway!

Our little expedition reached Trondheim in the evening and found that due to a convention, there was not a single room to be had for miles. Finally, a kind hotel clerk made some calls and found a pension for us about ten miles south of town.

We stayed the night there, and the next morning, after a delightful smorgasbord-style breakfast, my father explained in broken Swedish to the Norwegian innkeeper that we would spend the day in Trondheim trying to pick up the faint trail of our Aunes and Hegstads. We headed off to town and enjoyed a bountiful day at the archives easily unearthing lots of information about my father's family. Armed with this knowledge, my father photographed the row house where Andrew and Kari once lived and even the church where Andrew was baptized.

We returned to the pension that evening, flushed with the thrill of learning so much about our forebears. The Norwegian innkeeper tapped on our door shortly after and stood there with a glint in her eye. She explained she had just attended a community meeting where she talked to a neighbor whose maiden name happened to be Hegstad. The innkeeper had mentioned the names of our family to her, just out of curiosity.

We looked at her, wondering where this was all going. She stepped aside and beckoned to a woman clutching a photo album. This woman was the granddaughter of Kari Hegstad's half sister. In her album she had photographs of all four of the Hegstad siblings who had emigrated and their babies as well. She had a family tree that contained the name of my father's father, who was born in Minnesota and had never set foot in Norway. At the bottom of the chart were the names of my father himself and most of his siblings.

So here was a living relative of ours with an album full of people she had never met, living a mile away from the inn, the only place available in the whole region. Because the day at the archives had been so fruitful, because she had the pictures to prove the connection, and because we happened on the innkeeper who was able to make this link, we found our Norwegian cousins. To our family at least, this experience shows how blind luck can sometimes lead you home!

—*Colleen Aune Moore, Illinois*

# It Just Showed Up

*A*lthough I'd long been interested in family history, a trip to the Family History Library wasn't on my to-do list. Whenever someone would ask if I wanted to go, they were met with a polite, "Thank you, no." That was until a friend invited me to join her for a research jaunt. This time, for some unknown reason, the answer was yes. Living in Utah, I have easy access to this incredible genealogical resource, but because I'm African-American, I wasn't optimistic about finding much there.

Having accepted the invitation, I called my mother to verify a few family facts, including my deceased father's birth date. During the conversation, she casually mentioned that she had something I might want. Every family seems to have a designated keeper of family photos and documents, and in our family, that was me. For this reason, my mother thought I might be interested in seeing a paper written in my father's hand. I certainly was, but my interest soared when I learned that the paper contained a list of all his siblings and their birth dates, as well as the birth and death dates of his parents! I couldn't imagine why my mother hadn't shared this treasure before, so I asked her where it came from. She had no idea and said it had just showed up a week or two earlier. Strange, since Dad had been dead more than thirty years.

With this unexpected windfall of information, I ventured to the library with the intent of learning more about my father's family. A couple of helpful people at the information desk told me how to get started, but after many tedious, unproductive hours of scouring microfilm, I had found nothing. Patience has never been my most apparent quality and I was getting fed up with this whole research idea.

As a last resort, I pushed myself away from the microfilm viewer and offered up a silent prayer: "God, if I'm supposed to be doing this, if you want me to find something, it's got to be soon or I'm outta here!"

After my silent prayer, I returned to the viewer. In one last attempt, I pushed the button to advance the film and waited. When the machine stopped, I glanced at the page. To my absolute amazement, there in front of me was the entry for my grandfather's family. For the second time, the information I was seeking had "just showed up."

I remember clearly the emotion of the moment when I found that census record. I cried with joy, relief, and gratitude. Words can't really describe the feeling that comes when the link is made to your family and its history. In the beginning I hadn't held out much hope, but the message was clear: I was doing what I was supposed to be doing.

—*Darius Gray, Utah*

# Postcard Guard

*M*y mother started me with a postcard collection when I was about six by giving me a stack she had been accumulating for some years. I played with them as a child, but always kept the postcards together as a collection. Over the years, my mother's initial contribution grew to more than four thousand!

When I first became seriously interested in genealogy around 1981, I decided to look through the postcards to see if there might be anything of genealogical interest in there. By this time, I was in the Marine Corps and lived in Austin, Texas, many miles south of my Chicago roots. Having moved several times during my service, I had learned to travel light so my postcard collection was the only family documentation I had with me to peruse. I knew that some of the ones given to me by my mother had been sent to her by assorted family members, so I hoped to find a clue or two in their faded scribbles.

After digging through endless piles, I came across one that felt rather thick. Upon closer inspection, I discovered it was actually two postcards stuck together. When I carefully pulled them apart, out fell the original 1848 marriage certificate of my great-great-grandparents, Jesse Cook and Deborah Mahala Tallman! It was folded, but otherwise in perfect condition. Those sturdy postcards had protected this precious document in spite of years of handling and traveling.

What a start to my genealogical quest! I have always felt that my ancestors were watching over me that day and guided me to this long-concealed treasure. If they were aiming to inspire me, it certainly worked!

—*Liz Kelley Kerstens, CGRS, Michigan*

*One of the many postcards from Liz Kerstens's collection.*

To all whom these presents may come

I George E, Tiffin one of the Justices of the
Peace of the County of Monmouth do hereby
Certify that I have this day Joined
Jesse Cook and Deborah M, Tallman in
the holy bands of Matrimony.

Given under my hand and seal this
21st day of May in the year of our Lord one
Thousand eight hundred and Forty eight

George E, Tiffin Justice.

*1848 marriage certificate discovered lodged between two postcards.*

# Welcome Interruption

As I was sitting at a fiche reader at the Western Australian Genealogical Society one day, the conversation of the woman next to me penetrated into my thoughts. I generally try to blank out nearby conversations, but tidbits seeped in despite my efforts to concentrate on my own research.

The woman was a newcomer and was being helped by one of the society's volunteers. They were chatting about the little bit of information she had and I heard the names Carr and Robinson mentioned. These names don't appear in my family tree, but just the week before, I had tripped across them in a letter I received from a woman who lives more than 500 miles away. She and I were comparing notes about our common ancestors and her letter included her whole family tree, with the names Carr and Robinson featuring prominently.

I tentatively butted into their conversation, feeling a bit silly since I didn't really know what they were discussing from the snippets I had heard. They looked at me blankly as I tried to explain what I thought they wanted and what I thought I had. I pulled out the relevant pages, about four of them, and they stared in amazement. The pages contained precisely the information this woman was seeking!

I stopped feeling silly, and we all kept laughing and saying, "I don't believe it." The volunteer copied the pages for her and I felt *so* good to have been the lucky messenger who was in the right place at the right time to make the connection. You can be sure that from now on, I won't be quite so hesitant to interrupt strangers' conversations!

—*Robyn Wilton, Australia*

# Signs of Illness

*My* husband had spent fifteen years searching for information on his great-great-great-grandfather, George Parker. No one in the extended Kentucky family had any idea where he was born or where he had died. Every effort to find the mysterious George Parker had failed and it seemed our research was permanently stalled.

Several years ago, my husband and I attended my forty-fifth high school reunion in Evansville, Indiana. On the return trip to Georgia, I was suddenly overcome by a severe case of motion sickness. I was so ill that it became apparent we had to immediately turn off the interstate and park, rather than waiting for a rest stop or gas station. An empty, undeveloped exit came up right away, and we pulled off onto a lonely country road.

Just ahead was a dusty one-lane road that led to a small churchyard with a tree-shaded parking area. We stopped so I could get out of the car. Once I started feeling a little better, my husband decided to investigate the cemetery; he knew some of his relatives were from Webster County, Kentucky, which is where we happened to find ourselves. Now recuperating from the sudden bout of nausea, I heard him call out excitedly to me, "Betsy . . . come here! You'll never guess what I found!"

I walked over to where he was standing and looked down at the tombstone in front of him. It read, "George Parker, born January 11, 1824, died August 10, 1904." Our elusive prey had evaded us for years, but must have gotten tired of hiding. I'm sure he meant no harm, but what a way to get our attention!

—*Betsy Stansberry, Georgia*

# Christmas Present

*W*hen my mother was eleven and her only sister was four, a fire consumed their house the day after Christmas, taking the young girls' mother and destroying all of the family's possessions. As people somehow manage to do, the family picked up the pieces and the girls grew to adulthood and raised their own families.

About twenty-five years ago, I began searching for my family's roots, but gave up due to plain frustration. Seven years ago, I decided to resume the search as my aunt had become depressed since my mother's death and seemed desperate to reassemble whatever shreds of her family she could.

Hoping they might be able to help me, I called a Texas genealogical society in the area the family had moved to in 1901. The woman who responded said she didn't have much to offer beyond the name of a woman from Arizona who had signed the society's guest book noting that she was researching the same surname. I allowed a flicker of hope to come alive in me!

With some sleuthing, I found this woman in Arizona, but it turned out to be a dead end, as there was obviously no connection between our families. Trying to ease my obvious disappointment, she told me she had kept a napkin with the name of a woman from New Jersey whom she had met while doing research in Texas two years earlier. Maybe this woman would share my line.

I wasn't especially optimistic, but seeing no alternatives, decided to find and contact this woman. I called her and—success! We *were* related, but the best was yet to come! As luck would have it, she had just received a photo of her grandfather and mine as small boys *the day before I called her*! She sent it overnight to me, and I immediately overnighted it to my aunt with no warning that it was coming.

On Christmas Eve, she received a piece of the past that had been stolen from her all those years before in that post-Christmas fire. It was the first photo she had ever seen of her father as a youngster. All the other photos of the first forty years of his life had burned in the fire. This little Christmas miracle was easily the best present I have ever given her.

—*Marti Walker, Oklahoma*

# Serendipity Delayed

*O*ne of the goals of our trip to Ireland last year was to find more information about the family of our Irish ancestor who had emigrated in 1880. We had no idea of how we could do this. All we knew was that he had left from Goulane Townland, Castlegregory Parish, on the Dingle Peninsula in County Kerry.

We spent our first night at a B&B near the Dublin Airport. The next morning at breakfast, we were exchanging small talk with some Americans who had been traveling around Ireland. When we told them that we were heading to County Kerry, they suggested that we go the long way and visit the ruins at Glendalough in County Wicklow. This was, in hindsight, our first serendipitous event.

We followed their suggestion. That evening, while watching television in the living room of our B&B in Wicklow, we told a fellow guest of our plan. She gave us a card for what she called the most comfortable B&B in the Castlegregory area. Serendipitous link #2.

In Castlegregory, we met the young hostess of the recommended B&B. She had been brought up in Goulane, but wasn't well acquainted with the family we were researching. She advised that they had all died, but she would arrange for us to visit an elderly couple who still lived in Goulane, right next door to the farm that had been owned by our ancestors. We visited the couple in their little house, but were not successful in getting any meaningful information. We considered it a very nice experience and left it at that, not knowing that link #3 had taken place.

Several months later, back home in Alabama, I was surfing the Internet and happened onto an Irish bulletin board site. I listed our ancestor's name and location. I have no idea now which bulletin board it was, but it was link #4.

A month after posting that query, we found a strange e-mail message. It was from the son of the elderly couple. He lives in a different part of Ireland and had learned from his folks that some Americans had been there asking questions about the deceased residents of the farm next door. We told him that we were indeed that couple.

He advised us that as a youth, he had worked on his own family's genealogy, and that on the possibility that there had been some long-ago marriages between his ancestors and the people next door, he had compiled information about our ancestors too. It turned out that there was no such connection, but he had kept his research notes anyway. Would we like a copy of those notes? I should say so!

A new cluster of ancestors in one fell swoop! Just luck? I don't think so. Saint Serendipity had scored again!

—*Edmond Campbell, Alabama*

# Careful Where You Look!

$\mathcal{M}$y husband and I were on a trip to Wales. While walking through Havorfordwest, Pembrokeshire, we saw a museum and decided to go in. Once inside, I spotted an archives room. I told my husband to go on in the museum and I would try my luck in the archives. I knew that I had a great-great-great-grandmother who was born in Pembrokeshire, and hoped that I might find some information on her family.

The room was very small and crowded. I waited for a few minutes and no one paid any attention to me, so I looked around and found a card file with the alphabet on the outside. I had no idea what it contained, but wanted to do *something*! I pulled out the file for "B" and found a card with the name John Broad and the correct birth date for my great-great-great-grandfather and some other information that made no sense to me.

I got the attention of the archivist and told him I had found my ancestor but didn't know what the card was telling me. He replied, "Those are records for jail inmates. People don't usually start searching there!"

It seems that the building was the local jail in former times. The card indicated that John Broad was turned in by the local vicar for abandoning his family, an offense that was fairly common at the time due to the shortage of work that caused laborers to travel in search of a living wage. When he saw that I wasn't put off by this inauspicious beginning, the archivist took an interest in my research and helped me find a record of marriage of John Broad to Margaret Gibbon. I had not known Margaret's last name until then.

Ironically, it was the fact that he had temporarily abandoned his family that led me to my great-great-great-grandfather's family. For that, I can overlook his jailbird past!

—*Jeanette Smith, Arizona*

# A Different Kind of Valentine's Day

*M*y great-grandmother, Annie Barnett Justice, was born in New York in 1838, the daughter of Scottish immigrants. The man she would marry, Anton Moore, was a German immigrant who arrived in the United States in 1857.

Annie's mother died in 1840 before Annie had reached her second birthday. Her father, John Justice, moved Annie and her two sisters to Wisconsin where he raised his three daughters with the help of relatives. The oldest of John's daughters, Isabella, was the first to marry in 1861, but died soon after with the birth of her first child in 1862. The baby girl, Belle, survived, and her two aunts, still unmarried at the time, cared for her.

Anton Mohr—later Anton Moore—served in the Civil War for the Wisconsin Militia. Several years after completing his service, he married Annie Justice and agreed to raise her five-year-old niece as his own daughter, as Annie was the only "mother" she had known. Belle's father gave Anton $200—all he had—to help with the cost of raising her and headed out West, essentially dropping out of her life. We still have a tintype picture of charming little Belle taken when she was about three or four years old.

Anton and Annie had seven children of their own, and moved from Wisconsin to Iowa. Anton was a successful farmer who believed in hard work. Annie was a fine seamstress who sewed all the clothes for her brood. We have a picture of the family when all the children were teenagers. Annie had sewn the clothes for all nine people in the photo. Two sons became vets, and the youngest, Charles, became a farmer in Canada. He was my grandfather.

I became interested in genealogy when my sons were young, and began trying to piece together bits of family history. Fortunately, our family had always kept in contact with our Iowa cousins. When one of them, Raymond Moore, came to Canada for a visit, he brought along a box of old family documents. He knew of my interest in genealogy and thought I might like to browse through the papers.

Until then, I had no idea of what had happened to Belle, or any notion of how to go about finding her as I had no married name for her. That was about to change. One of the documents I received was Anton's will, dated 1913. In it, he requested that the funeral expenses be paid first, and the rest go to his wife. The third item in the will caught my attention:

> *After the death of my said wife, should she outlive me, I direct that the funeral expenses of my said wife be paid out of my estate and after the payment is made, I direct that $300 be given to Isabel Y. Smith, a niece of my said wife, living in Valentine, Nebraska.*

I was thrilled to realize that I now had the clue I needed to pick up little Belle's trail, but would I be able to find her descendants? I was researching in the early 1980s, so about seventy years had passed since the will was written. Deciding I had nothing to lose, I wrote a letter addressed to "Any living descendent of Belle Y. Smith, Valentine, Nebraska."

Three weeks later, a letter arrived from Valentine, Nebraska. The first line said, "I am the granddaughter of Belle Yaw Smith and the postmistress at Valentine, Nebraska." To my amazement, the lady who wrote, Ruth Harmes, was also a genealogist. The last branch of the family was found!

In a letter, Anton made the comment that he wanted the first money in his estate to go to Belle because "she never was a burden to us and brought us nothing but joy." Although blended families are common now, they weren't in the 1860s; and it is a tribute to this man that he was so kind, both in life and in death, to a child who was not his own. I think he would have been very pleased that Belle has found her place in the family tree.

—*Marilyn Pottage, Canada*

# Restoring a Sampler Restored My Family

*D*uring an Advanced Genealogy Elderhostel in Salt Lake City, my husband of Swedish descent found ancestors by the handful while I labored to find a scrap of information about my mother's elusive Irish ancestors.

With only two hours left on the last day of the Elderhostel, my frustration was so great that I threw up my hands and decided to just "go graze a bit." I wandered down one of the many aisles in the United States stacks in the Family History Library. Looking up at the thousands of books, I selected one at random. It contained the minutes of a Quaker Meeting in Delaware. There were no Quakers in my family and none of my ancestors came from Delaware, but I opened the book anyway, again at random.

There on the page in front of me were two generations of Olivers, a branch of my mother's family. I was certain because the names and dates exactly matched those on a sampler I had just sent for expert cleaning and remounting. The sampler had been worked by Catharine Oliver, my great-great-great-grandmother, in 1807.

I had no inkling that there were Quakers from Delaware in my family line. Up to this point, all my research had led me to the "certain" conclusion that all of my ancestors were from New York, New Jersey, and Pennsylvania and were either Episcopalian or Presbyterian. I think that perhaps this discovery was my great-great-great-grandmother's way of thanking me for taking good care of her handiwork!

—*Sinclair Craven Malm, Washington*

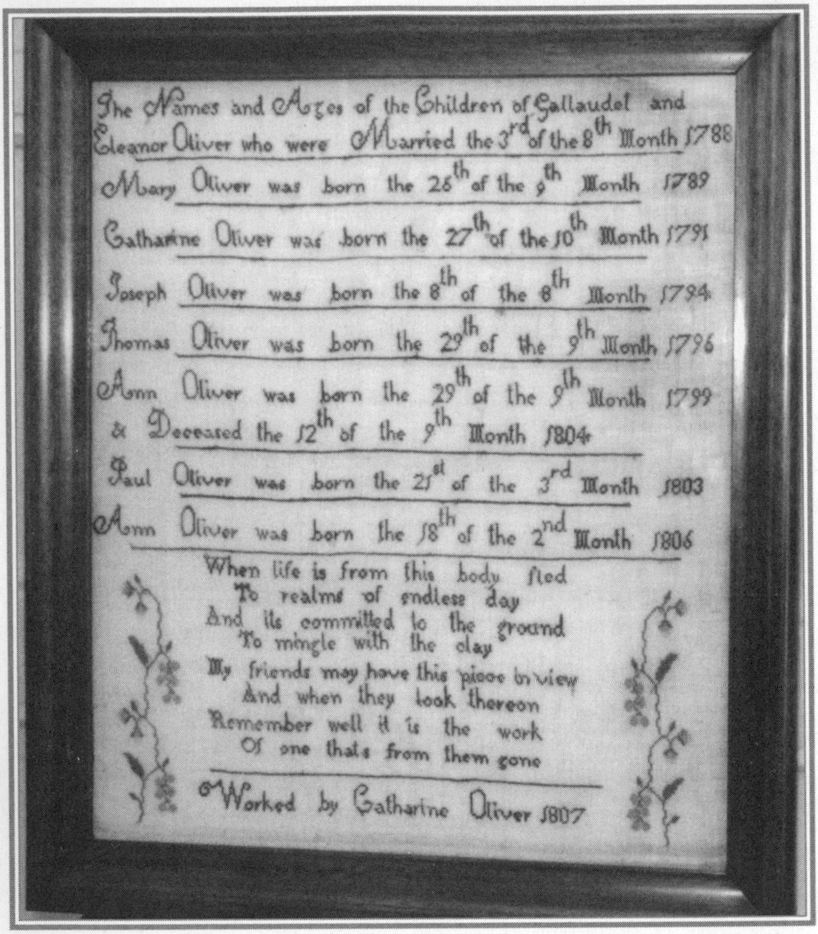


*Recently restored 1807 sampler of the Oliver family.*

# Timing Is Everything

$\mathscr{I}$ had spent more than a week in Pennsylvania giving one final push to my research effort so I could finish my family history book. In spite of all my digging, my father's half brother remained elusive, so I reluctantly resolved to complete the book without the details of his life. Although my father thought a great deal of his much-older half sibling, I knew almost nothing about him. I wasn't sure he had ever married or where he might have lived, and could find no clue of what had happened to him. My family had moved to Florida in 1958, and after my dad died in 1972 at age forty-nine, the families lost touch.

On the day of my departure, I had about three hours until I had to catch my plane, so I decided to sneak in one last bit of research. I dropped by the library in Uniontown, Pennsylvania, which was conveniently located on the way to the airport. I randomly picked up a book on cemeteries and it flipped open to La Fayette Cemetery. My eyes were immediately drawn to a listing for John Murray—my elusive half uncle! I knew it was the right John Murray because the birth date matched.

La Fayette Cemetery was also on my way to the airport, so I decided to push my luck with one more unscheduled stop. When I arrived, I saw that it was huge. Realizing that I would never find his grave without directions, I went to the cemetery office to ask for help.

The office was quiet, with just the secretary and one other visitor. When I asked for the burial record of John Murray, the other woman looked at me rather oddly and said, "You don't mean John L. Murray by any chance, do you?"

I said, "Yes, why?"

She replied, "He was my grandfather."

While the stunned secretary retrieved the obituary and burial record for me, I went out to my car and brought in the draft of my manuscript. My newly discovered cousin Virginia and I stood in the office looking it over. She said her family had just been talking about genealogy a few days before. They never knew who her grandfather's parents were, and she was amazed that I should show up with all the answers. She kept repeating, "I'm not believing this . . ."

The secretary copied the portion of my manuscript that pertained to Virginia's branch of the family and Virginia told me everything I needed to know to finish my book. With promises to keep in touch, I dashed out of the cemetery and managed, with precision timing, to just catch my flight!

—*Donna Murray Allen, Florida*

# Copier Cousins

$\mathscr{A}$ few years ago, my husband and I moved from California to Whidbey Island, Washington, where we settled in and I began working at a local drugstore. One day a man came into the store to do some copying. After he left, another customer came in to use the same machine and found a paper the first man had accidentally left behind. I inspected the paper to see if there was any information that would help identify the person who had left it.

Upon reading it, I let out a yell that brought coworkers running. You see, on the paper was the family tree of my grandmother!

Unfortunately, there was no information to help me locate the mystery man himself—who, I reasoned, must be a cousin of some sort. I was frustrated for myself, but felt especially sorry for him, as I know leaving papers behind is a genealogist's nightmare. All I could do was wait and hope he returned.

It took ten days for the man to come back to the store to do more copying. I wasn't even sure it was the same person, but I approached, asked some questions that probably made him think I was a psychic, and we made the connection. My great-grandmother and his grandmother were sisters, making us second cousins once removed. I was astonished as I had no idea that any part of my family had ever resided on Whidbey Island.

My copier cousin Frank introduced me to his wife and even invited me to spend the fourth of July together with his eight children and grandchildren. The rest of the country was celebrating independence, but I was celebrating my newfound family!

—*Dana Price Griffin, Washington*

# Blooming Ink

*W*hen I was young, my great-aunt Katie Mossy told me that when her sister, Loretta, died, she had lived to be older than any other Kelly in our family. Her brother, Uncle Albert Kelly, told me that, too. They bragged that now that my Grandma Loretta was gone, they were the oldest Kellys who had ever lived.

Many years later, while researching our family tree, I found that they were right. Through census records and newspaper obituaries, I found that all but one of our Kellys perished in their late twenties or early thirties of malaria, fevers, nephritis, or one of the other diseases prevalent in turn-of-the-century New Orleans.

The amount of information I gathered about family members grew scarcer the farther back in time I searched. Families of Irish immigrants were poor and mostly illiterate, so there was not much to find regarding my more distant ancestors. I found my family links dwindling as I hopped backward from child to parent to grandparent, with the trail finally growing cold with my great-great-grandmother, Mary Kelly.

As it was, time had erased her very existence, and the only acknowledgment the past allowed my grandmother's grandmother was a single line in the census records, stating simply that her name was Mary, wife of Timothy Kelly, born in 1839 in Ireland. These few facts were the single thread that connected me to my distant past, since ten years later, all trace of Mary Kelly was gone, and her husband was listed in the census as a widower.

New Orleans is an old city and a historical center, so the library is well stocked with records going back 250 years. There are many items of interest to a genealogist, and one day, I came upon a roll of microfilm with the burial records of a Catholic cemetery.

When I loaded the roll of microfilm onto the reader, I discovered that the film had been loaded on the reel backward, so that as I unspooled it, the back pages of the book appeared first. These pages were blank. As I kept unwinding the film, I noticed that the pages were waterlogged, as if the book had been damaged in a flood. I unreeled further, until I found that on the pages that had been used, the ink had bloomed upward as each page became soaked, smudging everything in its path. I kept going, until I reached the first page from the back where the water had stopped rising. This was the last page in the book that still had any writing left on it.

I scanned up from the bottom of the page, following the spread of the water stain toward the top, until I saw the last record in the cemetery register that had been spared from the flood. It was Mary Kelly's.

—*Dr. Colleen Fitzpatrick, California*

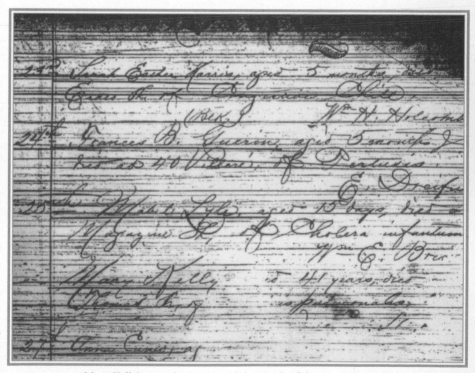

*Mary Kelly's record just escaped the reach of the water damage.*

# Permissions

Special thanks to KBYU and all the contributors who were so generous in providing photographs. Grateful acknowledgment is made to the following for permission to reprint previously published material:

"She Wanted Herself Known," written by Cathy Corcoran, appeared in the August 7, 1992, issue of *Patriot Ledger* of Quincy, Massachusetts. Reprinted with permission. Pages 6-8

"Looking for Margaret," written by Elizabeth Pope, appeared in the June 19, 1999, issue of the *St. Petersburg Times*. Reprinted by permission. Pages 41-42

"In Europe, Many Observe Memorial Day Every Day," written by Dr. Daniel Kortenkamp, appeared in the May 23, 1997, issue of the *Dubuque Telegraph Herald*. Reprinted by permission. Pages 133-135

"Let Me Explain," written by Monica Bennett, appeared in the August 3, 1999, issue of *Ancestry Daily News*. Reprinted by permission. Pages 142-143

"Finding My Father," written by Susan Hadler, appeared in the October 1998 issue of *Washingtonian* and the February 1999 issue of *Reader's Digest*. Reprinted with permission of both publications. Pages 195-197

"Postcard Guard," excerpted from Chapter 5, *Psychic Roots, Further Adventures in Serendipity & Intuition in Genealogy*, by Henry Z Jones Jr., copyright ©1997. Reprinted by permission of Genealogical Publishing Co., Inc. Pages 220-221

"Serendipity and the SS *Aurania*," written by Edward F. Holden, appeared in the January/February 1999 issue of *Ancestry*. Reprinted by permission. Pages 226-227

Excerpts from *Missing Links* and *Rootsweb Review*, edited by Myra Vanderpool Gormley and Julia M. Case. Reprinted by permission.

"Genealogical Records, Invaluable Aid to Marrow Donor Search," written by Pamelia S. Olson, first appeared in the January/February 1993, issue of *Heritage Quest,* issue #43, pages 16–18. Reprinted with permission. Pages 43-44

"Little White Lies" is adapted from the video "Piana," produced by The Brothers Gallup (bros-gallup@juno.com) about their roots-seeking journey to Sicily. Used with permission. Pages 117-118

"Remembrance & Reunion, Overseas Search Brings Mother, Twins Together," written by Carole Rafferty, appeared in the March 28, 1999, issue of *San Jose Mercury News*. Copyright ©1999 San Jose Mercury News. All rights reserved. Reproduced with permission. Use of this material does not imply endorsement of the *San Jose Mercury News*. Pages 32-34

Photo in "Diary of a Diary Quest," taken by Paul Barker, appeared in "Many miracles help Utahn discover her Irish ancestors" in the July 25, 1999, issue of *Deseret News*. Used with permission. Page 108

Photo in "A Dash of Larceny" appeared in "Barbette, Planning Writing Career, Enters San Quentin" in February 21, 1929 issue of the *San Francisco Chronicle*. Used with permission. Page 182

Photo in "Bi-Coastal Bible" taken by Chuck Brown, appeared in "Finding Family Bible Was a Genealogist's Dream" in May 21, 1999 issue of the *St. Croix Courier.* Used with permission. Page 162

# Acknowledgments

*For encouraging, tolerating, brainstorming, humoring, and other-wise supporting*—Stacy Neuberger, Seton Shields, Ray Freson, George Smolenyak, Barbara Smolenyak, Ann Harding, Diane Ganze, Laura Tinsley, Ellen Shew, Bob Holland, Bob Wiktor, Janet Winter, Peggy White, Brian Smolenyak.

*For being the catalyst for all this*—Saro Nakashian and Stephanie Ririe.

*For inviting me into their sandbox and letting me play with their toys*—Marcy Brown, Diena Simmons, John Reim, Matt Whitaker, Craig Steiner, Jim Tyrrell, Jim Dearden, Liz Thomas, Jon Anderson, Eric Young, Gene Ashbrook, Mary Jo Conder, Joe Pia, Christopher Brown, Kristina Bordon, Chris Bowman, Katy Rees, and the entire KBYU/Wisteria gang; also, Jack Ford and Pam Kawi.

*For pioneering the study of genealogical serendipity and having the courage to "out" the subject*—Henry Z Jones Jr., author of *Psychic Roots* and *More Psychic Roots.*

*For their guidance, patience, and enthusiasm through the publishing process*—Linda Konner, Ed Walters, Carrie Lewis, Aimee Adams, Keith Rainville, Daria Perreault, and Robin Witkin.

*For their contributions to genealogy and invaluable assistance with this book*—Myra Gormley, Julie Case, Dick Eastman, Cyndi Howells, Mark Howells, Rhonda McClure, Juliana Smith, Elizabeth Pope, Carole Rafferty, Halvor Moorshead, Joanne Todd Rabun, Bradley W. Steuart.

*For their assistance with both the series and the book*—The Family History Library, *Ancestry*, *Ancestry Daily News*, Rootsweb, *Missing Links*, *Rootsweb Review*, *Heritage Quest*, *Family Chronicle*, *Eastman's Online Genealogy Newsletter.*

*For their genealogical generosity*—All those who shared their stories, whether they appear in these pages or not. I wish I could have included five hundred!

We'd like to hear about your own genealogical stories of serendipity, kindness, and connection, and possibly use them for an upcoming sequel. Please send a brief summary of your experience to:

*In Search of Our Ancestors*
Adams Media Corporation
260 Center Street
Holbrook, MA 02343 U.S.A.
or
*www.honoringourancestors.com*

MEGAN SMOLENYAK is an international marketing consultant who has been researching her family history since she was in the sixth grade. Smolenyak has appeared on *Today* with Jack Ford (a second cousin) and is the lead researcher of the PBS series *Ancestors*. She has also published dozens of articles in genealogical publications and business magazines and delivers seminars and workshops on genealogical subjects.